THE PELICAN SHAKESPEARE

GENERAL EDITOR ALFRED HARBAGE

THE SECOND PART OF

KING HENRY THE FOURTH

WILLIAM SHAKESPEARE

THE SECOND PART OF KING HENRY THE FOURTH

EDITED BY ALLAN G. CHESTER

PENGUIN BOOKS

Penguin Books
625 Madison Avenue
New York, New York 10022

First published in *The Pelican Shakespeare* 1957
This revised edition first published 1970
Reprinted 1972, 1974, 1977, 1979

Library of Congress catalog card number: 70-97746

Printed in the United States of America by
Kingsport Press, Inc., Kingsport, Tennessee
Set in Monotype Ehrhardt

CONTENTS

PUBLISHER'S NOTE

Soon after the thirty-eight volumes forming *The Pelican Shake-speare* had been published, they were brought together in *The Com-plete Pelican Shakespeare*. The editorial revisions and new textual features are explained in detail in the General Editor's Preface to the one-volume edition. They have all been incorporated in the present volume. The following should be mentioned in particular:

The lines are not numbered in arbitrary units. Instead all lines are numbered which contain a word, phrase, or allusion explained in the glossarial notes. In the occasional instances where there is a long stretch of unannotated text, certain lines are numbered in italics to serve the conventional reference purpose.

The intrusive and often inaccurate place-headings inserted by early editors are omitted (as is becoming standard practise), but for the convenience of those who miss them, an indication of locale now appears as first item in the annotation of each scene.

In the interest of both elegance and utility, each speech-prefix is set in a separate line when the speaker's lines are in verse, except when these words form the second half of a pentameter line. Thus the verse form of the speech is kept visually intact, and turned-over lines are avoided. What is printed as verse and what is printed as prose has, in general, the authority of the original texts. Departures from the original texts in this regard have only the authority of editorial tradition and the judgment of the Pelican editors; and, in a few instances, are admittedly arbitrary.

SHAKESPEARE AND
HIS STAGE

William Shakespeare was christened in Holy Trinity Church, Stratford-upon-Avon, April 26, 1564. His birth is traditionally assigned to April 23. He was the eldest of four boys and two girls who survived infancy in the family of John Shakespeare, glover and trader of Henley Street, and his wife Mary Arden, daughter of a small landowner of Wilmcote. In 1568 John was elected Bailiff (equivalent to Mayor) of Stratford, having already filled the minor municipal offices. The town maintained for the sons of the burgesses a free school, taught by a university graduate and offering preparation in Latin sufficient for university entrance; its early registers are lost, but there can be little doubt that Shakespeare received the formal part of his education in this school.

On November 27, 1582, a license was issued for the marriage of William Shakespeare (aged eighteen) and Ann Hathaway (aged twenty-six), and on May 26, 1583, their child Susanna was christened in Holy Trinity Church. The inference that the marriage was forced upon the youth is natural but not inevitable; betrothal was legally binding at the time, and was sometimes regarded as conferring conjugal rights. Two additional children of the marriage, the twins Hamnet and Judith, were christened on February 2, 1585. Meanwhile the prosperity of the elder Shakespeares had declined, and William was impelled to seek a career outside Stratford.

The tradition that he spent some time as a country

teacher is old but unverifiable. Because of the absence of records his early twenties are called the "lost years," and only one thing about them is certain – that at least some of these years were spent in winning a place in the acting profession. He may have begun as a provincial trouper, but by 1592 he was established in London and prominent enough to be attacked. In a pamphlet of that year, *Groats-worth of Wit*, the ailing Robert Greene complained of the neglect which university writers like himself had suffered from actors, one of whom was daring to set up as a playwright:

. . . an vpstart Crow, beautified with our feathers, that with his *Tygers hart wrapt in a Players hyde*, supposes he is as well able to bombast out a blanke verse as the best of you: and beeing an absolute *Iohannes fac totum*, is in his owne conceit the onely Shake-scene in a countrey.

The pun on his name, and the parody of his line "O tiger's heart wrapped in a woman's hide" (*3 Henry VI*), pointed clearly to Shakespeare. Some of his admirers protested, and Henry Chettle, the editor of Greene's pamphlet, saw fit to apologize:

. . . I am as sory as if the originall fault had beene my fault, because my selfe haue seene his demeanor no lesse ciuill than he excelent in the qualitie he professes: Besides, diuers of worship haue reported his vprightnes of dealing, which argues his honesty, and his facetious grace in writting, that approoues his Art. (Prefatory epistle, *Kind-Harts Dreame*)

The plague closed the London theatres for many months in 1592–94, denying the actors their livelihood. To this period belong Shakespeare's two narrative poems, *Venus and Adonis* and *The Rape of Lucrece*, both dedicated to the Earl of Southampton. No doubt the poet was rewarded with a gift of money as usual in such cases, but he did no further dedicating and we have no reliable information on whether Southampton, or anyone else, became his regular patron. His sonnets, first mentioned in 1598 and published without his consent in 1609, are intimate without being

8

explicitly autobiographical. They seem to commemorate the poet's friendship with an idealized youth, rivalry with a more favored poet, and love affair with a dark mistress; and his bitterness when the mistress betrays him in conjunction with the friend; but it is difficult to decide precisely what the "story" is, impossible to decide whether it is fictional or true. The true distinction of the sonnets, at least of those not purely conventional, rests in the universality of the thoughts and moods they express, and in their poignancy and beauty.

In 1594 was formed the theatrical company known until 1603 as the Lord Chamberlain's men, thereafter as the King's men. Its original membership included, besides Shakespeare, the beloved clown Will Kempe and the famous actor Richard Burbage. The company acted in various London theatres and even toured the provinces, but it is chiefly associated in our minds with the Globe Theatre built on the south bank of the Thames in 1599. Shakespeare was an actor and joint owner of this company (and its Globe) through the remainder of his creative years. His plays, written at the average rate of two a year, together with Burbage's acting won it its place of leadership among the London companies.

Individual plays began to appear in print, in editions both honest and piratical, and the publishers became increasingly aware of the value of Shakespeare's name on the title pages. As early as 1598 he was hailed as the leading English dramatist in the *Palladis Tamia* of Francis Meres:

As *Plautus* and *Seneca* are accounted the best for Comedy and Tragedy among the Latines, so *Shakespeare* among the English is the most excellent in both kinds for the stage: for Comedy, witnes his *Gentlemen of Verona*, his *Errors*, his *Loue labors lost*, his *Loue labours wonne* [at one time in print but no longer extant, at least under this title], his *Midsummers night dream*, & his *Merchant of Venice*; for Tragedy, his *Richard the 2, Richard the 3, Henry the 4, King Iohn, Titus Andronicus*, and his *Romeo and Iuliet*.

The note is valuable both in indicating Shakespeare's prestige and in helping us to establish a chronology. In the second half of his writing career, history plays gave place to the great tragedies; and farces and light comedies gave place to the problem plays and symbolic romances. In 1623, seven years after his death, his former fellow-actors, John Heminge and Henry Condell, cooperated with a group of London printers in bringing out his plays in collected form. The volume is generally known as the First Folio.

Shakespeare had never severed his relations with Stratford. His wife and children may sometimes have shared his London lodgings, but their home was Stratford. His son Hamnet was buried there in 1596, and his daughters Susanna and Judith were married there in 1607 and 1616 respectively. (His father, for whom he had secured a coat of arms and thus the privilege of writing himself gentleman, died in 1601, his mother in 1608.) His considerable earnings in London, as actor-sharer, part owner of the Globe, and playwright, were invested chiefly in Stratford property. In 1597 he purchased for £60 New Place, one of the two most imposing residences in the town. A number of other business transactions, as well as minor episodes in his career, have left documentary records. By 1611 he was in a position to retire, and he seems gradually to have withdrawn from theatrical activity in order to live in Stratford. In March, 1616, he made a will, leaving token bequests to Burbage, Heminge, and Condell, but the bulk of his estate to his family. The most famous feature of the will, the bequest of the second-best bed to his wife, reveals nothing about Shakespeare's marriage; the quaintness of the provision seems commonplace to those familiar with ancient testaments. Shakespeare died April 23, 1616, and was buried in the Stratford church where he had been christened. Within seven years a monument was erected to his memory on the north wall of the chancel. Its portrait bust and the Droeshout engraving on the title page of the First Folio provide the only likenesses with an established claim to authenticity. The best verbal vignette was written by his rival Ben Jonson, the more impressive for being imbedded in a context mainly critical:

> ... I loved the man, and doe honour his memory (on this side idolatry) as much as any. Hee was indeed honest, and of an open and free nature: had an excellent Phantsie, brave notions, and gentle expressions.... (*Timber or Discoveries*, ca. 1623–30)

*

The reader of Shakespeare's plays is aided by a general knowledge of the way in which they were staged. The King's men acquired a roofed and artificially lighted theatre only toward the close of Shakespeare's career, and then only for winter use. Nearly all his plays were designed for performance in such structures as the Globe – a three-tiered amphitheatre with a large rectangular platform extending to the center of its yard. The plays were staged by daylight, by large casts brilliantly costumed, but with only a minimum of properties, without scenery, and quite possibly without intermissions. There was a rear stage gallery for action "above," and a curtained rear recess for "discoveries" and other special effects, but by far the major portion of any play was enacted upon the projecting platform, with episode following episode in swift succession, and with shifts of time and place signaled the audience only by the momentary clearing of the stage between the episodes. Information about the identity of the characters and, when necessary, about the time and place of the action was incorporated in the dialogue. No place-headings have been inserted in the present editions; these are apt to obscure the original fluidity of structure, with the emphasis upon action and speech rather than scenic background. (Indications of place are supplied in the footnotes.) The acting, including that of the youthful apprentices to the profession who performed the parts of women, was highly skillful, with a premium placed upon grace of gesture and beauty of diction. The audiences, a cross section of the general public, commonly numbered a thousand, sometimes more than two thousand. Judged by the type of plays they applauded, these audiences were not only large but also perceptive.

THE TEXTS OF THE PLAYS

About half of Shakespeare's plays appeared in print for the first time in the folio volume of 1623. The others had been published individually, usually in quarto volumes, during his lifetime or in the six years following his death. The copy used by the printers of the quartos varied greatly in merit, sometimes representing Shakespeare's true text, sometimes only a debased version of that text. The copy used by the printers of the folio also varied in merit, but was chosen with care. Since it consisted of the best available manuscripts, or the more acceptable quartos (although frequently in editions other than the first), or of quartos corrected by reference to manuscripts, we have good or reasonably good texts of most of the thirty-seven plays.

In the present series, the plays have been newly edited from quarto or folio texts, depending, when a choice offered, upon which is now regarded by bibliographical specialists as the more authoritative. The ideal has been to reproduce the chosen texts with as few alterations as possible, beyond occasional relineation, expansion of abbreviations, and modernization of punctuation and spelling. Emendation is held to a minimum, and such material as has been added, in the way of stage directions and lines supplied by an alternative text, has been enclosed in square brackets.

None of the plays printed in Shakespeare's lifetime were divided into acts and scenes, and the inference is that the author's own manuscripts were not so divided. In the folio collection, some of the plays remained undivided, some were divided into acts, and some were divided into acts and scenes. During the eighteenth century all of the plays were divided into acts and scenes, and in the Cambridge edition of the mid-nineteenth century, from which the influential Globe text derived, this division was more or less regularized and the lines were numbered. Many useful works of reference employ the act–scene–line apparatus thus established.

Since this act–scene division is obviously convenient, but is of very dubious authority so far as Shakespeare's own structural principles are concerned, or the original manner of staging his plays, a problem is presented to modern editors. In the present series the act–scene division is retained marginally, and may be viewed as a reference aid like the line numbering. A star marks the points of division when these points have been determined by a cleared stage indicating a shift of time and place in the action of the play, or when no harm results from the editorial assumption that there is such a shift. However, at those points where the established division is clearly misleading – that is, where continuous action has been split up into separate "scenes" – the star is omitted and the distortion corrected. This mechanical expedient seemed the best means of combining utility and accuracy.

THE GENERAL EDITOR

INTRODUCTION

To Shakespeare and his contemporaries, the history of their country between the accession of Richard II in 1377 and the Battle of Bosworth Field in 1485 provided a double fascination. It was a period of stirring events – of rebellion and counter-rebellion, and of victories over enemies abroad. Shrewsbury and Agincourt were names as familiar and evocative to Shakespeare's audience as are Antietam and Gettysburg to Americans of our own day. Owen Glendower and Harry Hotspur and Henry Bolingbroke were as well-remembered as John Brown and Stonewall Jackson and Ulysses Grant. As with us, the events and the men had been misted over with the passage of time, and the facts of history had been transmuted into tradition and even legend. But to the Elizabethans this period meant something more than romantic history. It served also as a "mirror," as they themselves put it, wherein Elizabeth's England might perceive important truths having to do with theories of government, the responsibility of the monarch, the duty of the subject, and the evil consequences of rebellion.

In the light of this interest, and of the consequent vogue for dramatized history which flourished in the theatres of the 1590's, it is not surprising that Shakespeare wrote no fewer than eight plays dealing with this period of English history. Four of these – the three Henry VI plays and *Richard III* – were written early in his career, but the other four – *Richard II*, the two parts of *Henry IV*, and

Henry V – belong to the period when his craft as a dramatist and his lordship of language were approaching their full powers. *Richard II* portrayed the weakness and folly of Richard, his forced abdication, the succession of his cousin Henry Bolingbroke as King Henry IV, and finally the murder of Richard at Pomfret Castle. *1 Henry IV* told of the rebellion of those who had aided Henry to the throne and subsequently repented having done so, and of the defeat of the rebels at Shrewsbury; *2 Henry IV* told of the later rebellions, of the death of Henry IV, and of the succession of his son, Prince Hal, as Henry V. *Henry V*, treating of the English victories in France, brought the tetralogy to a close.

The present play, third in the tetralogy, was probably written in the spring of 1598 and produced on the stage immediately thereafter. It was printed in quarto in 1600, with a title page reading as follows: *The Second part of Henrie the fourth, continuing to his death, and coronation of Henrie the fift. With the humours of sir Iohn Falstaffe, and swaggering Pistoll. As it hath been sundrie times publikely acted by the right honourable, the Lord Chamberlaine his seruants. Written by William Shakespeare. London. Printed by V. S. for Andrew Wise, and William Aspley. 1600.* Unlike *1 Henry IV*, which went through six quarto editions between 1598 and 1622, *2 Henry IV* was not reprinted until it appeared in the First Folio of 1623. Whether it was originally conceived as an afterthought, designed to capitalize upon the great success of its predecessor, or whether Shakespeare had planned from the start two plays on the reign of Henry IV is a point on which authorities differ. In either case the two plays constitute a dramatic entity. When read consecutively, they tell a unified and dramatically satisfying story.

For the principal events and the broad character outlines of the historical personages in the Henry IV plays, Shakespeare drew chiefly upon one of his favorite books – Raphael Holinshed's *Chronicles of the History of England*.

He also levied to a certain extent upon other sources. He may have taken a hint or two from the chronicles of Edward Hall and John Stow. Some details of the exploits of the unregenerate Prince Hal he derived from Sir Thomas Elyot's *The Book Named the Governor* and from the old play called *The Famous Victories of Henry V*. In dealing with his source material, Shakespeare worked, here as always in his chronicle plays, as an artist, not as an historian. He telescoped chronology in the interest of compression – the historical period covered in *2 Henry IV* was ten years (1403–13), but the play conveys no impression of this lapse of time. He discarded historical details which were dramatically irrelevant, altered the ages of some of his characters, expanded or suppressed character traits. The result is imperfect history; the modern reader or playgoer derives from the plays only a vague or confused notion of chronology and the order of events. But Shakespeare was not exclusively concerned with what John Drinkwater has called "that vast mutability which is event"; he was concerned also with the wonder of personality and the dramatic interplay of one character with another. And of course with poetry.

In dramatizing the reign of Henry IV, Shakespeare was confronted with the difficulty that the character of the monarch himself was neither winsome nor essentially dramatic. In Richard II, the poet discovered a pathetic, perhaps a tragic figure; Henry IV, despite his grief for the conduct of a wayward son, was neither pathetic nor tragic. Henry V was a military hero; Bolingbroke, despite the victories which won and kept his throne, was not. Moreover, the historical Henry IV did not participate directly in some of the most significant events of the reign. Hence Shakespeare did not attempt to make the king the pivotal figure of the action. He wisely chose to focus much of our attention upon other characters. In *1 Henry IV* his problem was the less by reason of the presence in his sources of certain historical personages of indubitable dramatic value. Prince Hal, the rhapsodic Glendower, the madcap Harry Percy and his charming wife Kate – these could be developed on the stage as vital figures. Especially Hotspur, whose reckless dedication to his cause made him an admirable foil to the apparently dissolute Hal. The contrast and conflict between the two Harry's becomes the most dramatic element in the play, overshadowing the father–son situation between king and prince, and the audience feels that the play has reached a suitable climax with the death of Hotspur at Shrewsbury Field.

Even so, however, Shakespeare chose not to rely solely upon the historical personages supplied him by the chroniclers. He invented the character of Falstaff, perhaps the most memorable comic character in the whole range of English fiction. The literary historians have taught us that Shakespeare's Falstaff is the culmination of a long tradition of the braggart soldier in Renaissance drama. No doubt Shakespeare was in some measure indebted to the tradition. But into this *miles gloriosus* he breathed the breath of individual life, and with a stroke of dramatic genius made him the center of a rowdy crew which included the Prince of Wales. Falstaff is a braggart, a liar, a lecher, a drunkard, a scrounger, a thief. But he is more – much more. His triumphant gift for extricating himself from the consequences of his misdoings has understandably endeared him to generations of theatre-goers. It is not surprising that a statue of the gargantuan knight stands among the figures in the grounds of the Memorial Theatre at Stratford, the symbol of Shakespeare's genius for comedy.

In *2 Henry IV*, dealing with events of the last years of Henry's reign, Shakespeare found the historical material less tractable than in *1 Henry IV*. Hotspur and Glendower were gone, the former slain by Prince Hal at Shrewsbury, the latter historically unavailable for the central action. Kate Percy indeed survives to make a fine speech lamenting her mate that's lost and denouncing the pusillanimity of her father-in-law Northumberland. Among the historical personages there remained the king, Prince Hal, the three other sons of the king, and the principal noblemen of the rival factions. With these Shakespeare does the best that he can. He also builds up, with moderate success, the characters of Richard Scroop, Archbishop of York, and the Lord Chief Justice. The former, who played but a minor role in *1 Henry IV*, is here the central figure in the rebellion in the north. He becomes the symbol of one of the political ideas of the play, the dilemma of the subject who, though acknowledging the principle of the divine right of kings, is yet galled by the abuse of power and feels compelled to take action against it. The Chief Justice, too, emerges as a lively personality, wise, humorous, realistic, who serves also as the voice of private decency and public authority to denounce the excesses of Falstaff and the profligacy of the Prince of Wales.

As with the characters, so with the principal dramatic narrative. In *1 Henry IV* there was the heroic action at Shrewsbury, where Prince Hal could speak a valedictory for the dead Hotspur:

> Fare thee well, great heart.
> Ill-weaved ambition, how much art thou shrunk!
> When that this body did contain a spirit,
> A kingdom for it was too small a bound;
> But now two paces of the vilest earth
> Is room enough. This earth that bears thee dead
> Bears not alive so stout a gentleman.

The later years of Henry's reign saw no such gallantry as this. Instead there was the bloodless, treacherous betrayal of the rebels at Gaultree Forest, which can end with nothing more heroic than Prince John of Lancaster's

> Strike up our drums, pursue the scattered stray.
> God, and not we, hath safely fought to-day.
> Some guard these traitors to the block of death,
> Treason's true bed and yielder up of breath.

Apart from this, Shakespeare's historical sources provided him with little material more dramatic than reports on the progress of the wars, debates concerning policy and strategy, and the like. On the historical side, the high moments of the play come at the end of Act IV and in Act V, with the portrayal of the old king on his deathbed, his final unscrupulous advice to the Prince of Wales concerning foreign wars, his death, and the coronation and transformation of the new king.

It is not surprising that Shakespeare, thus confronted with a paucity of truly dramatic history, develops his nonhistorical personages and situations to the extent that they dominate the play. It has often been pointed out that in *1 Henry IV* the proportion of the historical plot to the Falstaff story is 1649 lines to 1305, or roughly 5 to 4. In *2 Henry IV* the proportion has become 1422 lines to 1760, almost the precise reverse. Even without such statistics to guide him, the reader or playgoer is well aware that in this play Falstaff is the central figure. He overshadows the king and Hal, and his cronies overshadow the noble personages in the play. The Falstaff of most of the action of *2 Henry IV* is quite the equal of the Falstaff of *1 Henry IV*. We may say of him, as he says of himself, "The brain of this foolish compounded clay-man is not able to invent anything that intends to laughter more than I invent or is invented on me. I am not only witty in myself, but the cause that wit is in other men."

But Shakespeare has here done more than sustain and enlarge the Falstaff of the earlier play. He has also developed and individualized the characters of Falstaff's boon companions, and from a mere sketch in one scene in *1 Henry IV* he has created the memorable comic figure of Mistress Quickly, hostess of a tavern which tradition (but not Shakespeare, save for the merest hint – "Doth the old boar feed in the old frank?") identifies with the Boar's Head, which in Shakespeare's time (but not in Henry's) stood hard by the parish church of St Michael in Eastcheap. Mistress Quickly, a forebear of Mrs Malaprop, has been guilty of most of the amiable sins, but she is redeemed by simplicity and kindness of heart.

Apart from these, Shakespeare in this play invents four comic personages who had no existence in the earlier play – swaggering Pistol, Doll Tearsheet, a lady of joy, and the country justices Shallow and Silence. Modern audiences may find the rantings of Pistol tiresome and the love passages between Doll and Falstaff tasteless. But the two justices remain as entertaining to-day as they were on Shakespeare's stage – Shallow garrulous and gullible, Silence with his weakness for wine and his snatches of old songs. Generations of scholars have seen in the comic figure of Shallow a lampoon on some justice of the peace of Shakespeare's acquaintance. Identifications have ranged from Sir Thomas Lucy of Charlecote, near Stratford, on whose preserves, according to unsupported tradition, the youthful Shakespeare was involved in a poaching escapade, to William Gardiner, justice of the peace in the county of Surrey, with whom Shakespeare quarrelled in 1596. None of the identifications convinces a judicious mind. But the richness of the Gloucestershire local color against which Shallow is portrayed and the particularity of his fictitious recollections of his student days at Clement's Inn go far to explain the persistent belief that Shakespeare drew Shallow from the life.

In assigning to Falstaff a dominant role in the Henry IV plays and bringing him into close association with Prince Hal, Shakespeare created for himself the problem of disposing of Falstaff after the prince had become king. In the end, Shakespeare causes the new king to reject Falstaff summarily:

> I know thee not, old man. Fall to thy prayers.
> How ill white hairs become a fool and jester!
> I have long dreamed of such a kind of man,
> So surfeit-swelled, so old, and so profane,
> But, being awaked, I do despise my dream.

Our sympathy goes out to Falstaff; his "Master Shallow, I owe you a thousand pound" has for us a poignancy which Shakespeare did not intend. Yet we cannot deny the necessity for the rejection. A play portraying the victories of Henry V was in the offing. Obviously the hero of Agincourt could not continue to consort with Falstaff and his crew. As a concession to Fat Jack's popularity with the audience, the Epilogue to the present play promises that Sir John will appear in the sequel. But he does not appear. We hear only the Hostess's account of his passage to "Arthur's bosom," and Pistol's muted epitaph, "Falstaff he is dead, / And we must earn [grieve] therefore."

No element in *2 Henry IV* has provoked more critical comment than the rejection of Falstaff. Most commentators have found it in their hearts to wish that the playwright had been able to dispose of old Jack in some way which would have permitted us to feel a greater admiration for the regenerate Hal. But an attentive reading will disclose the fact that Shakespeare has prepared us for the rejection. Nowhere in this play do we see Falstaff and the prince in the same kind of intimacy which marked their relationship in *1 Henry IV*. Indeed, except for the rejection scene they are together just once, in the tavern scene in which Falstaff, as in the famous Gad's Hill episode of *1 Henry IV*, is the victim of a princely joke. But the Gad's Hill episode ended on a note of friendly banter; here there is no banter. The prince's last words are

> By heaven, Poins, I feel me much to blame,
> So idly to profane the precious time....
> Give me my sword and cloak. Falstaff, good night.

We have been warned of what is to follow. We need not condemn Hal too severely. Good judgment would have taught Falstaff that the laws of England would *not* be at his commandment after the death of the old king, and delicacy would have forbidden him to obtrude himself so abruptly into Hal's new situation. But good judgment and delicacy were not among Falstaff's qualities. It is Falstaff, not the prince, who compels the rejection.

Falstaff has provoked roars of laughter from the theatregoers of almost four centuries. Usually it is the Falstaff of *1 Henry IV* who is presented on the stage. Occasionally, from Betterton's time to our own, actors and producers have ventured to condense both parts into a single play of manageable proportions. *2 Henry IV* is less frequently presented as a separate play and in its entirety. However, on those occasions when it is, audiences find the experience delightful, and critics are impressed anew with Shakespeare's skill in mounting history upon the stage.

University of Pennsylvania   ALLAN G. CHESTER

NOTE ON THE TEXT

The present edition is based on the quarto of 1600, which is believed to have been printed from Shakespeare's own manuscript and to supply a better text than the folio, although that of the latter is fuller. The list of characters has been added from the folio text, as well as certain passages evidently omitted from the quarto because they dwell at length upon the censorable subject of civil rebellion. (These are the bracketed lines, I, i, 166–79, 189–209; I, iii, 21–24, 36–55, 85–108; II, iii, 23–45; IV, i, 55–79, 103–39.) The quarto is not divided into acts and scenes, and the division here indicated marginally is that of the folio text, except that in the latter the first act contains five scenes owing to the Induction's being counted as a separate scene, and the fourth act contains only two scenes. The wording of the stage directions of the quarto has been retained, but the names of four characters who neither speak nor are referred to in the dialogue have been eliminated: "Fauconbridge" in the opening stage direction at I, iii; "Sir John Russell" in that at II, ii; "Bardolph" in that at IV, i; and "Kent" in that at IV, iv. In V, iv, "Sincklo" (presumably the actor taking the part) has been emended to "Beadle." Listed below are substantive departures from the quarto text, including additions from the folio other than those mentioned above. The adopted reading is given in italics followed by the quarto reading in roman.

The Actors' Names (printed at the end of the play in F)
Ind. *Induction* (i.e. the heading, F; omitted in Q) 35 *hold* (Theobald) hole (F; passage not in Q)
I, i, 126 *Too* (F) so 161 *Travers* (Capell) Umfr. 164 *Lean on your* (F) leaue on you 178 *brought* (F2) bring (F; passage not in Q) 183 *ventured,...proposed* (Capell) ventured...proposde,
I, ii, 19 *fledged* (F) fledge 35 *rascally* (F) rascal! 46 *Where's Bardolph?* (F; follows 'through it' in line above in Q) 47 *into* (F) in 92 *age* (F) an ague 114 *Falstaff* (F) Old. 161 *bear-herd* (F) Berod 165 *them, are* (F) the one 192–93 *and Prince Harry* (F; omitted in Q)
I, iii, 28 *on* (F) and 66 *a* (F) so, 79 *He ... Welsh* (F) French and Welch he leaues his back vnarmde, they 109 *Mowbray* (F) Bish.
II, i, 14 *and that* (F; omitted in Q) 21 *vice* (F) view 25 *continuantly* (F) continually 76 *Fie!* (F; omitted in Q) 158 s.d. (follows line 155 in Q) 162 *Basingstoke* (F) Billingsgate
II, ii, 15 *viz.* (F) with 21 *thy* (F) the *made a shift to* (F; omitted in Q) 77 *new* (F; omitted in Q) 80 *rabbit* (F) rabble 107 *borrower's* (Warburton) borrowed 122 *familiars* (F) family
II, iii, 11 *endeared* (F) endeere
II, iv, 12–13 *Dispatch ... straight* (F; assigned to 'Dra.' in Q) 13 s.d. (follows line 17 in Q) 14 *3. Drawer* (Alexander) *2 Drawer* (F) Francis (Q) 20 *2. Drawer* (F) Francis 106 *shall* (F) shall not 159 *Die* (F; omitted in Q) 202 *Ah* (F) a 205 *Ah,* (F) a 300 *him* (F) thee
III, ii, 25 *This ... cousin* (F) Coosin, this sir Iohn 53 *[Shallow] ... gentlemen* (F; assigned to 'Silence' in Q) 107 *Falstaff. Prick him* (F; printed as s.d. 'Iohn prickes him' after line 106 in Q) 131 *to* (F; omitted in Q) 186–87 *no more of that* (F; omitted in Q) 198 *Clement's Inn* (F) Clemham 216 *old* (F; omitted in Q) 277 *Master Shallow* (F; omitted in Q)
IV, i, 30 *Then, my lord,* (F; omitted in Q) 34 *rags* (F) rage 139 *indeed* (Theobald) and did (F; passage not in Q)
IV, ii, s.d. (follows IV, i, 226 in Q) 8 *man* (F) man talking 24 *Employ* (F) Imply 97 s.d. (follows line 96 in Q) 117 *and ... yours* (F; omitted in Q) 122 *these traitors* (F) this traitour

IV, iii, 2 *I pray* (F; omitted in Q)   40 *their* (Q catchword) there
41 *Caesar* (Theobald) cosin   77–82 (printed as prose in Q)   80
pray, (F; omitted in Q)

IV, iv, 32 *meting* (F) meeting   52 *Canst . . . that?* (F; omitted in Q)
94 *heaven* (F) heavens   104 *write* (F) wet   *letters* (F) termes
132 *Softly, pray* (F; omitted in Q)

IV, v, 13 *altered* (F) uttred   49 *How . . . grace?* (F; omitted in Q)
75 *The virtuous sweets* (F; omitted in Q)   81 *hath* (F) hands   107
Which (F) Whom   160 *worst of* (F) worse then   177 *O my son,*
(F; omitted in Q)

V, i, 21 *the other day* (F; omitted in Q)   *Hinckley* (F) Hunkley   43
but a very (F; omitted in Q)

V, ii, s.d. ('duke Humphrey, Thomas Clarence, Prince John,
Westmerland' also listed in Q)

V, iii, 17–22, 32–36, 44–46, 51–52, 71–73, 90–94, 97–104, 113–17,
124–25, 137–38 (printed as prose in Q)

V, iv, 5 *enough* (F; omitted in Q)   6 *lately* (F; omitted in Q)   11 *He*
(F) I

V, v, 5 *Robert* (F; omitted in Q)   15 *Shallow* (F) Pist.   17, 19
Shallow (Hanmer) Pist.   29 *all* (F; omitted in Q)   31–38
(printed as prose in Q)

Epi. 29–30 *and . . . queen* (F; follows line 14 in Q)

THE SECOND PART
OF KING HENRY
THE FOURTH

THE ACTORS' NAMES

Rumor, the Presenter
King Henry the Fourth
Prince Henry, afterwards crowned King Henry the Fifth
Prince John of Lancaster ⎫
Humphrey of Gloucester ⎬ sons to Henry IV and
Thomas of Clarence ⎭ brethren to Henry V

[Earl of] Northumberland ⎫
[Richard Scroop] the Archbishop of York │
[Lord] Mowbray │
[Lord] Hastings ⎬ opposites
Lord Bardolph │ against King
Travers │ Henry IV
Morton │
[Sir John] Coleville ⎭

[Earl of] Warwick ⎫
[Earl of] Westmoreland │
[Earl of] Surrey │
[Sir John Blunt] │
Gower ⎬ of the King's party
Harcourt │
Lord Chief Justice │
[His Servant] ⎭

[Robert] Shallow ⎫
Silence ⎬ both country justices

Davy, servant to Shallow
Fang and Snare, two sergeants

[Ralph] Mouldy ⎫
[Simon] Shadow │
[Thomas] Wart ⎬ country soldiers
[Francis] Feeble │
[Peter] Bullcalf ⎭

Poins
[Sir John] Falstaff
Bardolph
Pistol } *irregular humorists*
Peto
[Falstaff's] Page
Northumberland's Wife
Percy's Widow [Lady Percy]
Hostess Quickly
Doll Tearsheet
[A Dancer as] Epilogue
[Francis and other] Drawers, Beadle [and other Officers],
    Grooms [, Porter, Messenger, Soldiers, Lords, Attendants]

[Scene: *England*]

THE SECOND PART
OF KING HENRY
THE FOURTH

INDUCTION

Enter Rumor, painted full of tongues.

RUMOR
 Open your ears, for which of you will stop
 The vent of hearing when loud Rumor speaks?
 I, from the orient to the drooping west,
 Making the wind my post-horse, still unfold   4
 The acts commencèd on this ball of earth.
 Upon my tongues continual slanders ride,
 The which in every language I pronounce,
 Stuffing the ears of men with false reports.
 I speak of peace while covert enmity
 Under the smile of safety wounds the world.
 And who but Rumor, who but only I,
 Make fearful musters and prepared defense
 Whiles the big year, swoln with some other grief,
 Is thought with child by the stern tyrant war,
 And no such matter? Rumor is a pipe   15
 Blown by surmises, jealousies, conjectures,   16
 And of so easy and so plain a stop   17
 That the blunt monster with uncounted heads, 18
 The still-discordant wavering multitude,
 Can play upon it. But what need I thus

Ind.   **4** *still* ever   **15** *pipe* wind instrument   **16** *jealousies* suspicions   **17**
of...stop whose stops are so easily played upon   **18** *blunt* stupid

My well-known body to anatomize
22 Among my household? Why is Rumor here?
I run before King Harry's victory,
Who in a bloody field by Shrewsbury
25 Hath beaten down young Hotspur and his troops,
Quenching the flame of bold rebellion
Even with the rebels' blood. But what mean I
28 To speak so true at first? My office is
29 To noise about that Harry Monmouth fell
Under the wrath of noble Hotspur's sword,
And that the king before the Douglas' rage
32 Stooped his anointed head as low as death.
33 This have I rumored through the peasant towns
Between that royal field of Shrewsbury
35 And this worm-eaten hold of ragged stone,
Where Hotspur's father, old Northumberland,
37 Lies crafty-sick. The posts come tiring on,
And not a man of them brings other news
Than they have learned of me. From Rumor's tongues
They bring smooth comforts false, worse than true
    wrongs.   *Exit Rumor.*

I, i   *Enter the Lord Bardolph at one door.*
LORD BARDOLPH
Who keeps the gate here, ho?
        [Enter the Porter.]   Where is the earl?
PORTER
What shall I say you are?
LORD BARDOLPH   Tell thou the earl

---

22 *my household* i.e. the audience   **25** *Hotspur* Harry Percy, killed by the
Prince of Wales at Shrewsbury   **28** *office* function   **29** *Harry Monmouth*
the Prince of Wales (Prince Hal)   **32** *Stooped . . . death* was mortally
wounded   **33** *peasant towns* villages   **35** *hold* stronghold (Warkworth
Castle, seat of the Earl of Northumberland, where the action of the next
scene occurs)   **37** *crafty-sick* feigning sickness; *tiring on* riding until
exhausted
I, i Before Northumberland's castle (at Warkworth)

That the Lord Bardolph doth attend him here.

PORTER
His lordship is walked forth into the orchard.
Please it your honor, knock but at the gate,
And he himself will answer.
    Enter the Earl of Northumberland.

LORD BARDOLPH   Here comes the earl.
                                [Exit Porter.]

NORTHUMBERLAND
What news, Lord Bardolph? Every minute now
Should be the father of some stratagem.
The times are wild. Contention, like a horse
Full of high feeding, madly hath broke loose
And bears down all before him.

LORD BARDOLPH   Noble earl,
I bring you certain news from Shrewsbury.

NORTHUMBERLAND
Good, an God will!   13

LORD BARDOLPH   As good as heart can wish.
The king is almost wounded to the death;
And, in the fortune of my lord your son,
Prince Harry slain outright; and both the Blunts
Killed by the hand of Douglas. Young Prince John
And Westmoreland and Stafford fled the field;
And Harry Monmouth's brawn, the hulk Sir John,   19
Is prisoner to your son. O, such a day,
So fought, so followed, and so fairly won,
Came not till now to dignify the times
Since Caesar's fortunes!   23

NORTHUMBERLAND   How is this derived?
Saw you the field? Came you from Shrewsbury?

LORD BARDOLPH
I spake with one, my lord, that came from thence,
A gentleman well bred and of good name,

13 *an* if   19 *brawn* swine (referring to Falstaff's size and habits)   23 *fortunes*
successes

That freely rendered me these news for true.

NORTHUMBERLAND

Here comes my servant Travers, whom I sent
On Tuesday last to listen after news.

Enter Travers.

LORD BARDOLPH

30 My lord, I overrode him on the way,
And he is furnished with no certainties
32 More than he haply may retail from me.

NORTHUMBERLAND

Now, Travers, what good tidings comes with you?

TRAVERS

My lord, Sir John Umfrevile turned me back
With joyful tidings, and, being better horsed,
Outrode me. After him came spurring hard
37 A gentleman, almost forspent with speed,
That stopped by me to breathe his bloodied horse.
He asked the way to Chester, and of him
I did demand what news from Shrewsbury.
He told me that rebellion had bad luck
And that young Harry Percy's spur was cold.
With that, he gave his able horse the head,
And bending forward struck his armèd heels
Against the panting sides of his poor jade
Up to the rowel-head, and starting so
He seemed in running to devour the way,
48 Staying no longer question.

NORTHUMBERLAND   Ha! Again.
Said he young Harry Percy's spur was cold?
Of Hotspur Coldspur? That rebellion
Had met ill luck?

LORD BARDOLPH My lord, I'll tell you what.
If my young lord your son have not the day,
53 Upon mine honor, for a silken point

---

30 *overrode* overtook   **32** *haply* perhaps   **37** *forspent* exhausted   **48** *Staying* waiting for   **53** *point* lace for tying the breeches

I'll give my barony. Never talk of it.

NORTHUMBERLAND
  Why should that gentleman that rode by Travers
  Give then such instances of loss?

LORD BARDOLPH   Who, he?
  He was some hilding fellow that had stolen   57
  The horse he rode on, and, upon my life,
  Spoke at a venture. Look, here comes more news.
     Enter Morton.

NORTHUMBERLAND
  Yea, this man's brow, like to a title-leaf,   60
  Foretells the nature of a tragic volume.
  So looks the strand whereon the imperious flood
  Hath left a witnessed usurpation.   63
  Say, Morton, didst thou come from Shrewsbury?

MORTON
  I ran from Shrewsbury, my noble lord,
  Where hateful death put on his ugliest mask
  To fright our party.

NORTHUMBERLAND How doth my son and brother?
  Thou tremblest, and the whiteness in thy cheek
  Is apter than thy tongue to tell thy errand.
  Even such a man, so faint, so spiritless,
  So dull, so dead in look, so woebegone,
  Drew Priam's curtain in the dead of night,   72
  And would have told him half his Troy was burnt.
  But Priam found the fire ere he his tongue,
  And I my Percy's death ere thou report'st it.
  This thou wouldst say, 'Your son did thus and thus;
  Your brother thus. So fought the noble Douglas' –
  Stopping my greedy ear with their bold deeds.   78
  But in the end, to stop my ear indeed,
  Thou hast a sigh to blow away this praise,
  Ending with 'Brother, son, and all are dead.'

57 *hilding* worthless 60 *title-leaf* title page 63 *a witnessed usurpation* evidences of its destruction 72 *Priam* king of Troy 78 *Stopping* filling

MORTON
> Douglas is living, and your brother, yet;
> But, for my lord your son —

NORTHUMBERLAND   Why, he is dead.
> See what a ready tongue suspicion hath!
> He that but fears the thing he would not know
> Hath by instinct knowledge from others' eyes
> That what he feared is chancèd. Yet speak, Morton.
> Tell thou an earl his divination lies,
> And I will take it as a sweet disgrace
> And make thee rich for doing me such wrong.

MORTON
> You are too great to be by me gainsaid.
> Your spirit is too true, your fears too certain.

NORTHUMBERLAND
93   Yet, for all this, say not that Percy's dead.
> I see a strange confession in thine eye.
> Thou shakest thy head and hold'st it fear or sin
> To speak a truth. If he be slain, say so.
> The tongue offends not that reports his death
> And he doth sin that doth belie the dead,
> Not he which says the dead is not alive.
> Yet the first bringer of unwelcome news
101   Hath but a losing office, and his tongue
> Sounds ever after as a sullen bell,
> Rememb'red tolling a departing friend.

LORD BARDOLPH
> I cannot think, my lord, your son is dead.

MORTON
> I am sorry I should force you to believe
> That which I would to God I had not seen.
> But these mine eyes saw him in bloody state,
108   Rendering faint quittance, wearied and outbreathed,
> To Harry Monmouth, whose swift wrath beat down

---

93 *for* in spite of   **101** *losing office* thankless task   **108** *faint quittance* weak
return of blows

The never-daunted Percy to the earth,
From whence with life he never more sprung up.
In few, his death, whose spirit lent a fire 112
Even to the dullest peasant in his camp,
Being bruited once, took fire and heat away 114
From the best-tempered courage in his troops.
For from his metal was his party steeled,
Which once in him abated, all the rest
Turned on themselves, like dull and heavy lead.
And as the thing that's heavy in itself,
Upon enforcement flies with greatest speed,
So did our men, heavy in Hotspur's loss,
Lend to this weight such lightness with their fear
That arrows fled not swifter toward their aim
Than did our soldiers, aiming at their safety,
Fly from the field. Then was that noble Worcester
Too soon ta'en prisoner; and that furious Scot,
The bloody Douglas, whose well-laboring sword
Had three times slain the appearance of the king, 128
'Gan vail his stomach and did grace the shame 129
Of those that turned their backs, and in his flight,
Stumbling in fear, was took. The sum of all
Is that the king hath won, and hath sent out
A speedy power to encounter you, my lord,
Under the conduct of young Lancaster
And Westmoreland. This is the news at full.

NORTHUMBERLAND
For this I shall have time enough to mourn.
In poison there is physic; and these news,
Having been well, that would have made me sick,
Being sick, have in some measure made me well.
And as the wretch whose fever-weakened joints,
Like strengthless hinges, buckle under life,
Impatient of his fit, breaks like a fire

112 *In few* in few words 114 *bruited* reported 128 *the appearance . . . king*
noblemen disguised as the king 129 *'Gan . . . stomach* began to let his
courage fail; *grace* excuse

35

Out of his keeper's arms, even so my limbs,
144 Weakened with grief, being now enraged with grief,
145 Are thrice themselves. Hence, therefore, thou nice
crutch!
A scaly gauntlet now with joints of steel
147 Must glove this hand. And hence, thou sickly quoif!
148 Thou art a guard too wanton for the head
149 Which princes, fleshed with conquest, aim to hit.
Now bind my brows with iron, and approach
151 The ragged'st hour that time and spite dare bring
To frown upon the enraged Northumberland!
Let heaven kiss earth! Now let not Nature's hand
Keep the wild flood confined! Let order die!
And let this world no longer be a stage
To feed contention in a lingering act.
157 But let one spirit of the first-born Cain
Reign in all bosoms, that, each heart being set
On bloody courses, the rude scene may end,
And darkness be the burier of the dead!

[TRAVERS]
161 This strainèd passion doth you wrong, my lord.

LORD BARDOLPH
Sweet earl, divorce not wisdom from your honor.

MORTON
The lives of all your loving complices
Lean on your health, the which, if you give o'er
To stormy passion, must perforce decay.
166 [You cast the event of war, my noble lord,
And summed the account of chance, before you said,
168 'Let us make head.' It was your presurmise
169 That, in the dole of blows, your son might drop.

---

144 *grief . . . grief* pain . . . sorrow 145 *nice* effeminate 147 *quoif* nightcap
(or bandage) 148 *wanton* trifling 149 *fleshed* aroused, as a dog is aroused
from feeding on raw meat 151 *ragged'st* roughest 157 *spirit . . . Cain* i.e.
spirit of murder 161 *strainèd passion* outburst of feeling 166 *cast the event*
calculated the consequences 168 *make head* raise an army 169 *dole* chance
distribution

You knew he walked o'er perils, on an edge,
More likely to fall in than to get o'er.
You were advised his flesh was capable   172
Of wounds and scars and that his forward spirit
Would lift him where most trade of danger ranged.
Yet did you say, 'Go forth.' And none of this,
Though strongly apprehended, could restrain
The stiff-borne action. What hath then befallen,   ·   177
Or what hath this bold enterprise brought forth,
More than that being which was like to be?]   179

LORD BARDOLPH
We all that are engagèd to this loss   180
Knew that we ventured on such dangerous seas
That if we wrought out life 'twas ten to one.
And yet we ventured, for the gain proposed
Choked the respect of likely peril feared.   184
And since we are o'erset, venture again.
Come, we will all put forth, body and goods.

MORTON
'Tis more than time. And, my most noble lord,
I hear for certain, and dare speak the truth,
[The gentle Archbishop of York is up   189
With well-appointed powers. He is a man
Who with a double surety binds his followers.
My lord your son had only but the corpse,   192
But shadows and the shows of men, to fight.
For that same word 'rebellion' did divide
The action of their bodies from their souls,
And they did fight with queasiness, constrained,
As men drink potions, that their weapons only
Seemed on our side. But for their spirits and souls,
This word 'rebellion,' it had froze them up,

172 *advised* aware   177 *stiff-borne* obstinately carried out   179 *More ... be*
more than the event which you knew was a possibility   180 *engagèd to*
involved in   184 *respect* consideration   189–90 *is up ... powers* has taken
the field with a well-equipped army   192 *only ... corpse* only the bodies of
men whose hearts were not in the fight

As fish are in a pond. But now the bishop
Turns insurrection to religion.
Supposed sincere and holy in his thoughts,
He's followed both with body and with mind,
204 And doth enlarge his rising with the blood
205 Of fair King Richard, scraped from Pomfret stones;
206 Derives from heaven his quarrel and his cause;
Tells them he doth bestride a bleeding land,
208 Gasping for life under great Bolingbroke;
209 And more and less do flock to follow him.]

NORTHUMBERLAND
I knew of this before; but, to speak truth,
This present grief had wiped it from my mind.
Go in with me, and counsel every man
The aptest way for safety and revenge.
214 Get posts and letters, and make friends with speed.
Never so few, and never yet more need.   *Exeunt.*

*

I, ii   *Enter Sir John [Falstaff] alone, with his Page
bearing his sword and buckler.*

FALSTAFF Sirrah, you giant, what says the doctor to my
2   water?

PAGE He said, sir, the water itself was a good healthy
4   water; but, for the party that owed it, he might have
5   moe diseases than he knew for.

6 FALSTAFF Men of all sorts take a pride to gird at me. The
brain of this foolish compounded clay-man is not able
to invent anything that intends to laughter more than I
invent or is invented on me. I am not only witty in myself, but the cause that wit is in other men. I do here walk

204 *enlarge his rising* extend the significance of his revolt 205 *Pomfret*
Pomfret Castle, where Richard II was murdered 206 *Derives from heaven*
gives a religious significance to 208 *Bolingbroke* Henry IV 209 *more and
less* high and low 214 *make* collect
I, ii A London street 2 *water* urine 4 *owed* owned 5 *moe* more 6 *gird*
jeer

before thee like a sow that hath overwhelmed all her
litter but one. If the prince put thee into my service for
any other reason than to set me off, why then I have no
judgment. Thou whoreson mandrake, thou art fitter to   14
be worn in my cap than to wait at my heels. I was never
manned with an agate till now. But I will inset you   16
neither in gold nor silver, but in vile apparel, and send
you back again to your master, for a jewel – the juvenal, 18
the prince your master, whose chin is not yet fledged. I   19
will sooner have a beard grow in the palm of my hand
than he shall get one off his cheek, and yet he will not
stick to say his face is a face-royal. God may finish it   22
when he will, 'tis not a hair amiss yet. He may keep it
still at a face-royal, for a barber shall never earn sixpence 24
out of it; and yet he'll be crowing as if he had writ man   25
ever since his father was a bachelor. He may keep his
own grace, but he's almost out of mine, I can assure   27
him. What said Master Dombledon about the satin for
my short cloak and my slops?   29

PAGE He said, sir, you should procure him better as-
surance than Bardolph. He would not take his band and   31
yours; he liked not the security.

FALSTAFF Let him be damned, like the glutton! Pray   33
God his tongue be hotter! A whoreson Achitophel! A   34
rascally yea-forsooth knave! To bear a gentleman in   35
hand, and then stand upon security! The whoreson
smooth-pates do now wear nothing but high shoes, and   37

---

14 *mandrake* a root popularly supposed to resemble a man   16 *manned ...
agate* served by a man as small as a carved agate stone   18 *juvenal* young
man   19 *fledged* covered with down   22, 24 *face-royal* a pun centering
around a coin, the royal (worth 10s.), with the king's face stamped on it   25
writ man attained manhood   27 *grace* (1) title of address ('your grace'), (2)
favor   29 *slops* wide breeches   31 *Bardolph* one of Falstaff's cronies, not to
be confused with Lord Bardolph; *band* bond   33 *glutton* i.e. Dives, referred to in Luke xvi, 24   34 *Achitophel* the adviser of Absalom (2 Samuel
xv–xvii)   35–36 *bear ... in hand* encourage   37 *smooth-pates* city trades-
men, who wore their hair short   37–38 *high shoes ... keys* (tokens of
prosperity and rank)

38   bunches of keys at their girdles; and if a man is through
with them in honest taking up, then they must stand
upon security. I had as lief they would put ratsbane in

41   my mouth as offer to stop it with security. I looked 'a
should have sent me two-and-twenty yards of satin, as I
am a true knight, and he sends me security. Well, he

44   may sleep in security, for he hath the horn of abundance,
and the lightness of his wife shines through it. And yet

46   cannot he see, though he have his own lanthorn to light
him. Where's Bardolph?

47   PAGE He's gone into Smithfield to buy your worship a
horse.

49   FALSTAFF I bought him in Paul's, and he'll buy me a
horse in Smithfield. An I could get me but a wife in the

51   stews, I were manned, horsed, and wived.

Enter Lord Chief Justice [and Servant].

52   PAGE Sir, here comes the nobleman that committed the
prince for striking him about Bardolph.

54   FALSTAFF Wait close; I will not see him.

CHIEF JUSTICE What's he that goes there?

SERVANT Falstaff, an't please your lordship.

57   CHIEF JUSTICE He that was in question for the robbery?

SERVANT He, my lord. But he hath since done good service at Shrewsbury, and, as I hear, is now going with
some charge to the Lord John of Lancaster.

CHIEF JUSTICE What, to York? Call him back again.

SERVANT Sir John Falstaff!

FALSTAFF Boy, tell him I am deaf.

38–40 *if . . . security* if a man has ordered a suit of clothes on promise of
future payment, they demand security before making delivery   **41** *'a* he
44 *horn of abundance* the horn of the cuckold   **46** *lanthorn* lantern (the pun
is that the wife's lightness shines in the cuckold's horn)   **47** *Smithfield* a
famous market   **49** *Paul's* St Paul's Cathedral (the nave of which was often
used as a labor exchange)   **51** *stews* brothels; *manned . . . wived* (the sense is
that a man who gets his horse at Smithfield, his servant at Paul's, and his wife
in the stews will get a poor bargain in each case)   **52** *committed* committed to
prison (see V, ii, 70n.)   **54** *close* close by   **57** *in question* under judicial
examination

PAGE You must speak louder; my master is deaf.

CHIEF JUSTICE I am sure he is, to the hearing of anything good. Go, pluck him by the elbow; I must speak
with him.

SERVANT Sir John!

FALSTAFF What! A young knave, and begging! Is there 69
not wars? Is there not employment? Doth not the king
lack subjects? Do not the rebels need soldiers? Though
it be a shame to be on any side but one, it is worse shame
to beg than to be on the worst side, were it worse than
the name of rebellion can tell how to make it.

SERVANT You mistake me, sir.   75

FALSTAFF Why, sir, did I say you were an honest man?
Setting my knighthood and my soldiership aside, I had
lied in my throat if I had said so.

SERVANT I pray you, sir, then set your knighthood and
your soldiership aside and give me leave to tell you you
lie in your throat if you say I am any other than an
honest man.

FALSTAFF I give thee leave to tell me so! I lay aside that 82
which grows to me! If thou get'st any leave of me, hang
me; if thou tak'st leave, thou wert better be hanged. You
hunt counter. Hence! Avaunt!   85

SERVANT Sir, my lord would speak with you.

CHIEF JUSTICE Sir John Falstaff, a word with you.

FALSTAFF My good lord! God give your lordship good
time of day. I am glad to see your lordship abroad. I
heard say your lordship was sick. I hope your lordship
goes abroad by advice. Your lordship, though not clean 91
past your youth, have yet some smack of age in you,
some relish of the saltness of time in you; and I most
humbly beseech your lordship to have a reverent care of
your health.

69 *knave* boy   75 *mistake* misunderstand   82–83 *that . . . to me* i.e. my
knighthood, which is an integral part of myself   85 *counter* in the wrong
direction (with play upon 'the Counter,' a debtors' prison)   91 *by advice*
i.e. with your physician's approval

CHIEF JUSTICE Sir John, I sent for you before your expedition to Shrewsbury.

FALSTAFF An't please your lordship, I hear his majesty is returned with some discomfort from Wales.

CHIEF JUSTICE I talk not of his majesty. You would not come when I sent for you.

FALSTAFF And I hear, moreover, his highness is fallen into this same whoreson apoplexy.

CHIEF JUSTICE Well, God mend him! I pray you, let me speak with you.

FALSTAFF This apoplexy, as I take it, is a kind of lethargy, an't please your lordship, a kind of sleeping in the blood, a whoreson tingling.

CHIEF JUSTICE What tell you me of it? Be it as it is.

109 **FALSTAFF** It hath it original from much grief, from study and perturbation of the brain. I have read the cause of
111 his effects in Galen. It is a kind of deafness.

CHIEF JUSTICE I think you are fallen into the disease, for you hear not what I say to you.

FALSTAFF Very well, my lord, very well. Rather, an't please you, it is the disease of not listening, the malady of not marking, that I am troubled withal.

117 **CHIEF JUSTICE** To punish you by the heels would amend the attention of your ears, and I care not if I do become your physician.

FALSTAFF I am as poor as Job, my lord, but not so patient. Your lordship may minister the potion of im-
122 prisonment to me in respect of poverty; but how I should be your patient to follow your prescriptions, the
124 wise may make some dram of a scruple, or indeed a scruple itself.

CHIEF JUSTICE I sent for you, when there were matters

---

109 *it original* its origin   **111** *Galen* Greek medical writer of the second century A.D.   **117** *by the heels* in the stocks (or in prison)   **122** *in respect* by reason   **124** *make . . . scruple* hesitate to admit ('dram' and 'scruple' are small weights used by apothecaries)

against you for your life, to come speak with me.   126

FALSTAFF As I was then advised by my learned counsel
in the laws of this land-service, I did not come.   128

CHIEF JUSTICE Well, the truth is, Sir John, you live in
great infamy.

FALSTAFF He that buckles himself in my belt cannot live
in less.

CHIEF JUSTICE Your means are very slender and your
waste is great.

FALSTAFF I would it were otherwise. I would my means
were greater and my waist slenderer.

CHIEF JUSTICE You have misled the youthful prince.

FALSTAFF The young prince hath misled me. I am the
fellow with the great belly, and he my dog.

CHIEF JUSTICE Well, I am loath to gall a new-healed   140
wound. Your day's service at Shrewsbury hath a little
gilded over your night's exploit on Gad's Hill. You may   142
thank the unquiet time for your quiet o'erposting that   143
action.

FALSTAFF My lord?

CHIEF JUSTICE But since all is well, keep it so. Wake
not a sleeping wolf.

FALSTAFF To wake a wolf is as bad as smell a fox.   147

CHIEF JUSTICE What! You are as a candle, the better
part burnt out.

FALSTAFF A wassail candle, my lord, all tallow. If I did   150
say of wax, my growth would approve the truth.   151

CHIEF JUSTICE There is not a white hair in your face
but should have his effect of gravity.   153

FALSTAFF His effect of gravy, gravy, gravy.

---

126 *for your life* for which your life might have been forfeit   128 *land-service*
military service   140 *gall* irritate   142 *your . . . on Gad's Hill* (a robbing
escapade of Falstaff and the prince; see *1 Henry IV*, II)   143 *o'erposting*
escape from the consequences of   147 *smell a fox* be suspicious   150 *wassail
candle* large candle used at feasts   151 *wax* a pun on (1) beeswax, (2) grow
153 *effect* outward sign

CHIEF JUSTICE You follow the young prince up and down like his ill angel.

157 FALSTAFF Not so, my lord. Your ill angel is light, but I hope he that looks upon me will take me without
159 weighing. And yet, in some respects, I grant, I cannot go. I cannot tell. Virtue is of so little regard in these
161 costermongers' times that true valor is turned bear-
162 herd. Pregnancy is made a tapster, and hath his quick
163 wit wasted in giving reckonings. All the other gifts appertinent to man, as the malice of this age shapes them, are not worth a gooseberry. You that are old consider not the capacities of us that are young; you do measure the heat of our livers with the bitterness of
168 your galls. And we that are in the vaward of our youth, I must confess, are wags too.

CHIEF JUSTICE Do you set down your name in the scroll
170 of youth, that are written down old with all the characters of age? Have you not a moist eye? A dry hand? A yellow cheek? A white beard? A decreasing leg? An increasing belly? Is not your voice broken? Your wind
174 short? Your chin double? Your wit single? And every part about you blasted with antiquity? And will you yet call yourself young? Fie, fie, fie, Sir John!

FALSTAFF My lord, I was born about three of the clock in the afternoon, with a white head and something a
179 round belly. For my voice, I have lost it with halloing and singing of anthems. To approve my youth further, I will not. The truth is, I am only old in judgment and
182 understanding; and he that will caper with me for a
183 thousand marks, let him lend me the money, and have at

---

157 *ill angel* a clipped coin   **159–60** *cannot go* cannot pass for currency   **161** *costermongers' times* i.e. materialistic times (a costermonger is a huckster of apples and other fruits)   **162** *Pregnancy* intellectual attainment   **163** *reckonings* tavern bills   **168** *vaward* vanguard   **170** *characters* (1) characteristics, (2) letters   **174** *single* poor, trivial   **179** *halloing* shouting to hounds   **182** *caper* compete in a dance   **183** *marks* coins worth 13s. 6d. apiece

him! For the box of the ear that the prince gave you, he gave it like a rude prince, and you took it like a sensible lord. I have checked him for it, and the young lion repents; marry, not in ashes and sackcloth, but in new silk and old sack.   187

CHIEF JUSTICE Well, God send the prince a better companion!

FALSTAFF God send the companion a better prince! I cannot rid my hands of him.

CHIEF JUSTICE Well, the king hath severed you and Prince Harry. I hear you are going with Lord John of Lancaster against the archbishop and the Earl of Northumberland.

FALSTAFF Yea, I thank your pretty sweet wit for it. But 194 look you pray, all you that kiss my lady Peace at home, 195 that our armies join not in a hot day, for, by the Lord, I take but two shirts out with me, and I mean not to sweat extraordinarily. If it be a hot day, and I brandish anything but a bottle, I would I might never spit white 199 again. There is not a dangerous action can peep out his head but I am thrust upon it. Well, I cannot last ever. But it was alway yet the trick of our English nation, if they have a good thing, to make it too common. If ye will needs say I am an old man, you should give me rest. I would to God my name were not so terrible to the enemy as it is. I were better to be eaten to death with a rust than to be scoured to nothing with perpetual motion.

CHIEF JUSTICE Well, be honest, be honest, and God bless your expedition!

FALSTAFF Will your lordship lend me a thousand pound to furnish me forth?

CHIEF JUSTICE Not a penny, not a penny. You are too

---

187 *sack* a Spanish wine   194 *wit* intellect   195 *look you pray* be sure to pray   199 *spit white* (meaning uncertain; in the light of Falstaff's character, the general sense is probably: May I never take another drink)

213   impatient to bear crosses. Fare you well. Commend me
to my cousin Westmoreland.

[Exeunt Chief Justice and Servant.]

215 FALSTAFF If I do, fillip me with a three-man beetle. A
man can no more separate age and covetousness than 'a
can part young limbs and lechery. But the gout galls the
one and the pox pinches the other, and so both the
219   degrees prevent my curses. Boy!

PAGE Sir?

FALSTAFF What money is in my purse?

222 PAGE Seven groats and two pence.

FALSTAFF I can get no remedy against this consumption
of the purse. Borrowing only lingers and lingers it out,
but the disease is incurable. Go bear this letter to my
Lord of Lancaster, this to the prince, this to the Earl of
Westmoreland, and this to old Mistress Ursula, whom I
have weekly sworn to marry since I perceived the first
white hair of my chin. About it. You know where to find
me. *[Exit Page.]* A pox of this gout! Or a gout of this
pox! For the one or the other plays the rogue with my
232   great toe. 'Tis no matter if I do halt; I have the wars for
233   my color, and my pension shall seem the more reasonable. A good wit will make use of anything. I will turn
235   diseases to commodity.   *[Exit.]*

*

I, iii   *Enter the Archbishop, Thomas Mowbray [Earl*
Marshal], the Lords Hastings and Bardolph.

ARCHBISHOP
Thus have you heard our cause and known our means;
And, my most noble friends, I pray you all,

---

213 *crosses* (1) afflictions, (2) coins stamped with a cross   215 *fillip* strike;
three-man beetle ram or pile driver requiring three men to lift it   219
prevent anticipate   222 *groats* coins worth 4d. apiece   232 *halt* limp   233
color excuse   235 *commodity* profit
I, iii The palace of the Archbishop of York

Speak plainly your opinions of our hopes.
And first, lord marshal, what say you to it?

MOWBRAY

I well allow the occasion of our arms,   5
But gladly would be better satisfied
How in our means we should advance ourselves   7
To look with forehead bold and big enough
Upon the power and puissance of the king.   9

HASTINGS

Our present musters grow upon the file   10
To five-and-twenty thousand men of choice;
And our supplies live largely in the hope   12
Of great Northumberland, whose bosom burns
With an incensèd fire of injuries.

LORD BARDOLPH

The question then, Lord Hastings, standeth thus:
Whether our present five-and-twenty thousand
May hold up head without Northumberland?

HASTINGS

With him, we may.

LORD BARDOLPH   Yea, marry, there's the point.
But if without him we be thought too feeble,
My judgment is, we should not step too far
[Till we had his assistance by the hand.
For in a theme so bloody-faced as this,   22
Conjecture, expectation, and surmise
Of aids incertain should not be admitted.]

ARCHBISHOP

'Tis very true, Lord Bardolph, for indeed
It was young Hotspur's case at Shrewsbury.   26

LORD BARDOLPH

It was, my lord, who lined himself with hope,   27
Eating the air on promise of supply,

---

5 *allow the occasion* admit the justification   7 *in* with   9 *puissance* power
10 *file* roll   12 *supplies* reinforcements   22 *theme* matter   26 *case* situation
27 *lined* reinforced

29 Flattering himself in project of a power
Much smaller than the smallest of his thoughts,
And so, with great imagination
Proper to madmen, led his powers to death
33 And winking leaped into destruction.

HASTINGS

But, by your leave, it never yet did hurt
To lay down likelihoods and forms of hope.

LORD BARDOLPH

36 [Yes, if this present quality of war,
Indeed the instant action, a cause on foot,
Lives so in hope as in an early spring
We see the appearing buds, which to prove fruit,
Hope gives not so much warrant as despair
That frosts will bite them. When we mean to build,
42 We first survey the plot, then draw the model.
43 And when we see the figure of the house,
Then must we rate the cost of the erection,
Which if we find outweighs ability,
What do we then but draw anew the model
47 In fewer offices, or at least desist
To build at all? Much more, in this great work,
Which is almost to pluck a kingdom down
And set another up, should we survey
The plot of situation and the model,
52 Consent upon a sure foundation,
53 Question surveyors, know our own estate,
How able such a work to undergo,
55 To weigh against his opposite. Or else]

29–30 *in . . . thoughts* in the foolish notion that his army was much larger than it was in fact   **33** *winking* shutting his eyes   **36–41** (an obscure passage; the sense is: Yes, but in this instance there is harm in over-optimism, just as there is harm in being overhopeful about the buds of early spring and forgetting the possibility of a killing frost)   **42** *model* plan   **43** *figure* design   **47** *offices* supplementary rooms for services   **52** *Consent* agree   **53** *surveyors* architects   **55** *his opposite* the opposition

We fortify in paper and in figures,   56
Using the names of men instead of men,
Like one that draws the model of a house
Beyond his power to build it, who, half through,
Gives o'er and leaves his part-created cost   60
A naked subject to the weeping clouds
And waste for churlish winter's tyranny.   62

HASTINGS
Grant that our hopes, yet likely of fair birth,
Should be still-born, and that we now possessed
The utmost man of expectation,
I think we are a body strong enough,
Even as we are, to equal with the king.

LORD BARDOLPH
What, is the king but five-and-twenty thousand?

HASTINGS
To us no more, nay, not so much, Lord Bardolph.
For his divisions, as the times do brawl,
Are in three heads: one power against the French,
And one against Glendower, perforce a third
Must take up us. So is the unfirm king
In three divided, and his coffers sound   74
With hollow poverty and emptiness.

ARCHBISHOP
That he should draw his several strengths together   76
And come against us in full puissance
Need not be dreaded.

HASTINGS   If he should do so,
[He leaves his back unarmed, the French and Welsh]
Baying him at the heels. Never fear that.

LORD BARDOLPH
Who is it like should lead his forces hither?   81

56 *We fortify in paper* our strength is all on paper   60 *part-created cost*
building unfinished because there was insufficient money to complete it
62 *churlish* violent   74 *sound* echo   76 *several* separate   81 *Who . . . should*
who is likely to

49

HASTINGS

> The Duke of Lancaster and Westmoreland.
> Against the Welsh, himself and Harry Monmouth.
84   But who is substituted 'gainst the French,
> I have no certain notice.

[ARCHBISHOP   Let us on,
> And publish the occasion of our arms.
> The commonwealth is sick of their own choice;
88   Their overgreedy love hath surfeited.
> An habitation giddy and unsure
> Hath he that buildeth on the vulgar heart.
91   O thou fond many, with what loud applause
92   Didst thou beat heaven with blessing Bolingbroke,
> Before he was what thou wouldst have him be!
94   And being now trimmed in thine own desires,
> Thou, beastly feeder, art so full of him
> That thou provok'st thyself to cast him up.
> So, so, thou common dog, didst thou disgorge
> Thy glutton bosom of the royal Richard;
> And now thou wouldst eat thy dead vomit up,
> And howl'st to find it. What trust is in these times?
> They that when Richard lived would have him die
> Are now become enamored on his grave.
103   Thou that threw'st dust upon his goodly head
> When through proud London he came sighing on
> After the admired heels of Bolingbroke
> Criest now, 'O earth, yield us that king again,
> And take thou this!' O thoughts of men accursed!
> Past and to come seems best, things present worst.]

[MOWBRAY]

109   Shall we go draw our numbers and set on?

HASTINGS

> We are time's subjects, and time bids be gone. *[Exeunt.]*

*

84 *substituted* delegated   88 *surfeited* overeaten   91 *fond many* foolish multitude   92 *beat heaven* assail heaven with prayers   94 *trimmed* dressed 103 *Thou* i.e. the multitude   109 *draw our numbers* assemble our troops

Enter Hostess of the Tavern and an Officer or two II, i
[Fang and another, followed by Snare].

HOSTESS Master Fang, have you entered the action? 1

FANG It is entered.

HOSTESS Where's your yeoman? Is't a lusty yeoman? 3
Will 'a stand to't?

FANG *[to Officer]* Sirrah, where's Snare?

HOSTESS O Lord, ay! Good Master Snare.

SNARE Here, here.

FANG Snare, we must arrest Sir John Falstaff.

HOSTESS Yea, good Master Snare, I have entered him
and all.

SNARE It may chance cost some of us our lives, for he will
stab.

HOSTESS Alas the day! Take heed of him. He stabbed me
in mine own house, and that most beastly. In good
faith, he cares not what mischief he does, if his weapon
be out. He will foin like any devil; he will spare neither 16
man, woman, nor child.

FANG If I can close with him, I care not for his thrust 18

HOSTESS No, nor I neither. I'll be at your elbow.

FANG An I but fist him once, an 'a come but within my 20
vice – 21

HOSTESS I am undone by his going. I warrant you, he's
an infinitive thing upon my score. Good Master Fang, 23
hold him sure. Good Master Snare, let him not 'scape.
'A comes continuantly to Pie Corner – saving your
manhoods – to buy a saddle; and he is indited to dinner 26
to the Lubber's Head in Lumbert Street, to Master 27
Smooth's the silkman. I pray you, since my exion is 28
entered and my case so openly known to the world, let

II, i Before an Eastcheap tavern **1** *Master Fang* the sheriff's sergeant;
entered the action begun the lawsuit **3** *yeoman* the sergeant's man **16**
foin thrust (with an indecent double meaning) **18** *close* grapple **20** *fist*
punch **21** *vice* grip **23** *infinitive* infinite (Mistress Quickly's spectacular
misuse of words will be obvious throughout); *score* tavern account **26**
indited i.e. invited **27** *Lubber's Head* Libbard's (Leopard's) Head (a shop
sign); *Lumbert* Lombard **28** *exion* action

him be brought in to his answer. A hundred mark is a
long one for a poor lone woman to bear, and I have
32 borne, and borne, and borne, and have been fubbed off,
and fubbed off, and fubbed off, from this day to that
day, that it is a shame to be thought on. There is no
honesty in such dealing, unless a woman should be
made an ass and a beast, to bear every knave's wrong.
37 Yonder he comes, and that arrant malmsey-nose knave,
Bardolph, with him. Do your offices, do your offices.
Master Fang and Master Snare, do me, do me, do me
your offices.

*Enter Sir John [Falstaff] and Bardolph, and the Boy
[Page].*

FALSTAFF How now! Whose mare 's dead? What's the
matter?

FANG Sir John, I arrest you at the suit of Mistress
Quickly.

FALSTAFF Away, varlets! Draw, Bardolph. Cut me off
44 the villain's head. Throw the quean in the channel.

HOSTESS Throw me in the channel! I'll throw thee in the
channel. Wilt thou? Wilt thou? Thou bastardly rogue!
47 Murder, murder! Ah, thou honeysuckle villain! Wilt
48 thou kill God's officers and the king's? Ah, thou honey-
49 seed rogue! Thou art a honeyseed, a man-queller, and a
woman-queller.

FALSTAFF Keep them off, Bardolph.

FANG A rescue! A rescue!

HOSTESS Good people, bring a rescue or two. Thou wo't,
wo't thou? Thou wo't, wo't ta? Do, do, thou rogue!
55 Do, thou hempseed!

56 PAGE Away, you scullion! You rampallian! You fustilar-
57 ian! I'll tickle your catastrophe.

---

32 *fubbed off* put off   37 *malmsey-nose* red-nosed from drinking wine   44
quean slut; *channel* gutter   47 *honeysuckle* i.e. homicidal   48 *honeyseed* i.e.
homicide   49 *man-queller* i.e. man-killer   55 *hempseed* gallows-bird   56
scullion kitchen wench; *rampallian* scoundrel; *fustilarian* frowsy fat woman
57 *catastrophe* backside

Enter Lord Chief Justice and his Men.

CHIEF JUSTICE
What is the matter? Keep the peace here, ho!

HOSTESS Good my lord, be good to me. I beseech you,
stand to me.   60

CHIEF JUSTICE
How now, Sir John! What are you brawling here?
Doth this become your place, your time and business?
You should have been well on your way to York.
Stand from him, fellow. Wherefore hang'st upon him?

HOSTESS O my most worshipful lord, an't please your
grace, I am a poor widow of Eastcheap, and he is
arrested at my suit.

CHIEF JUSTICE For what sum?

HOSTESS It is more than for some, my lord; it is for all,
all I have. He hath eaten me out of house and home; he
hath put all my substance into that fat belly of his. But I
will have some of it out again, or I will ride thee o' nights
like the mare.   73

FALSTAFF I think I am as like to ride the mare, if I have
any vantage of ground to get up.

CHIEF JUSTICE How comes this, Sir John? Fie! what
man of good temper would endure this tempest of
exclamation? Are you not ashamed to enforce a poor
widow to so rough a course to come by her own?

FALSTAFF What is the gross sum that I owe thee?

HOSTESS Marry, if thou wert an honest man, thyself and
the money too. Thou didst swear to me upon a parcel-   82
gilt goblet, sitting in my Dolphin chamber, at the round 83
table, by a sea-coal fire, upon Wednesday in Wheeson   84
week, when the prince broke thy head for liking his   85
father to a singing-man of Windsor, thou didst swear to
me then, as I was washing thy wound, to marry me and
make me my lady thy wife. Canst thou deny it? Did not

60 *stand to* help   73 *mare* nightmare   82 *parcel-gilt* partly gilded   83
Dolphin chamber (a room in her tavern)   84 *sea-coal* coal mined from sea-
coast veins; *Wheeson* Whitsun (Pentecost)   85 *liking* comparing

53

goodwife Keech, the butcher's wife, come in then and
90 call me gossip Quickly? Coming in to borrow a mess of
91 vinegar, telling us she had a good dish of prawns, whereby thou didst desire to eat some, whereby I told thee
93 they were ill for a green wound? And didst thou not,
when she was gone down stairs, desire me to be no more
so familiarity with such poor people, saying that ere long
they should call me madam? And didst thou not kiss me
and bid me fetch thee thirty shillings? I put thee now to
thy book-oath. Deny it, if thou canst.

FALSTAFF My lord, this is a poor mad soul, and she says
up and down the town that her eldest son is like you. She
101 hath been in good case, and the truth is, poverty hath
102 distracted her. But for these foolish officers, I beseech
you I may have redress against them.

CHIEF JUSTICE Sir John, Sir John, I am well acquainted
with your manner of wrenching the true cause the false
way. It is not a confident brow, nor the throng of words
that come with such more than impudent sauciness
108 from you, can thrust me from a level consideration. You
have, as it appears to me, practiced upon the easy-
yielding spirit of this woman, and made her serve your
uses both in purse and in person.

HOSTESS Yea, in truth, my lord.

CHIEF JUSTICE Pray thee, peace. Pay her the debt you
owe her and unpay the villainy you have done with her.
The one you may do with sterling money, and the other
116 with current repentance.

117 FALSTAFF My lord, I will not undergo this sneap without reply. You call honorable boldness impudent
sauciness. If a man will make curtsy and say nothing, he
is virtuous. No, my lord, my humble duty remembered,
I will not be your suitor. I say to you, I do desire de-
liverance from these officers, being upon hasty employ-

---

90 *gossip* (a familiar term of address) 91 *prawns* shrimps 93 *green* raw
101 *in good case* prosperous 102 *distracted her* driven her mad 108 *level*
unbiased 116 *current* genuine 117 *sneap* rebuke

ment in the king's affairs.

CHIEF JUSTICE You speak as having power to do wrong. But answer in the effect of your reputation, and satisfy the poor woman.   125

FALSTAFF Come hither, hostess.

Enter a Messenger [Gower].

CHIEF JUSTICE Now, Master Gower, what news?

GOWER

The king, my lord, and Harry Prince of Wales
Are near at hand. The rest the paper tells.

FALSTAFF As I am a gentleman.

HOSTESS Faith, you said so before.

FALSTAFF As I am a gentleman. Come, no more words of it.

HOSTESS By this heavenly ground I tread on, I must be fain to pawn both my plate and the tapestry of my dining-chambers.

FALSTAFF Glasses, glasses, is the only drinking. And for thy walls, a pretty slight drollery, or the story of the Prodigal, or the German hunting in water-work, is worth a thousand of these bed-hangings and these fly-bitten tapestries. Let it be ten pound, if thou canst. Come, an 'twere not for thy humors, there's not a better wench in England. Go, wash thy face, and draw the action. Come, thou must not be in this humor with me. Dost not know me? Come, come, I know thou wast set on to this.   137 138 139 142 143

HOSTESS Pray thee, Sir John, let it be but twenty nobles. I' faith, I am loath to pawn my plate, so God save me, la!   146

FALSTAFF Let it alone; I'll make other shift. You'll be a fool still.

HOSTESS Well, you shall have it, though I pawn my

---

125 *in . . . reputation* suitably for a man of your reputation **137** *Glasses . . . drinking* glasses, not metal tankards, are now fashionable **138** *drollery* comic picture **139** *water-work* water color **142** *humors* vagaries **143** *draw* withdraw **146** *nobles* coins worth 6s. 8d. each

gown. I hope you'll come to supper. You'll pay me all
together?

FALSTAFF Will I live? *[to Bardolph]* Go, with her, with
155 her. Hook on, hook on.

HOSTESS Will you have Doll Tearsheet meet you at
supper?

FALSTAFF No more words. Let's have her.
Exeunt Hostess and Sergeant [Fang, Bardolph, and others].

CHIEF JUSTICE I have heard better news.

FALSTAFF What's the news, my lord?

CHIEF JUSTICE Where lay the king last night?

GOWER At Basingstoke, my lord.

FALSTAFF I hope, my lord, all's well. What is the news,
my lord?

CHIEF JUSTICE Come all his forces back?

GOWER
No. Fifteen hundred foot, five hundred horse,
Are marched up to my lord of Lancaster,
Against Northumberland and the archbishop.

FALSTAFF
Comes the king back from Wales, my noble lord?

CHIEF JUSTICE
You shall have letters of me presently.
170 Come, go along with me, good Master Gower.

FALSTAFF My lord!

CHIEF JUSTICE What's the matter?

FALSTAFF Master Gower, shall I entreat you with me to
dinner?

GOWER I must wait upon my good lord here, I thank you,
good Sir John.

CHIEF JUSTICE Sir John, you loiter here too long, being
178 you are to take soldiers up in counties as you go.

FALSTAFF Will you sup with me, Master Gower?

---

155 *Hook on* stay with her and don't let her change   178 *take soldiers up*
recruit soldiers

CHIEF JUSTICE What foolish master taught you these
  manners, Sir John?
FALSTAFF Master Gower, if they become me not, he was
  a fool that taught them me. This is the right fencing   183
  grace, my lord – tap for tap, and so part fair.
CHIEF JUSTICE Now the Lord lighten thee! Thou art a   185
  great fool.   [Exeunt.]

*

Enter the Prince [Henry], and Poins, with others.   II, ii
PRINCE Before God, I am exceeding weary.
POINS Is't come to that? I had thought weariness durst
  not have attached one of so high blood.   3
PRINCE Faith, it does me, though it discolors the com-   4
  plexion of my greatness to acknowledge it. Doth it not
  show vilely in me to desire small beer?
POINS Why, a prince should not be so loosely studied as   7
  to remember so weak a composition.   8
PRINCE Belike, then, my appetite was not princely got,   9
  for, by my troth, I do now remember the poor creature,
  small beer. But indeed these humble considerations
  make me out of love with my greatness. What a disgrace
  is it to me to remember thy name! Or to know thy face
  to-morrow! Or to take note how many pair of silk
  stockings thou hast, viz. these, and those that were thy
  peach-colored ones! Or to bear the inventory of thy
  shirts, as, one for superfluity, and another for use! But   17
  that the tennis-court-keeper knows better than I; for it
  is a low ebb of linen with thee when thou keepest not

183-84 *right fencing grace* correct form in fencing   185 *lighten* enlighten
II, ii The London dwelling of Prince Henry   3 *attached* seized   4 *discolors
the complexion* makes me blush   7 *so loosely studied* such a careless student
8 *so weak a composition* such small beer, i.e. trifles   9 *got* begotten   17 *one
for superfluity* an extra one   17-20 *But . . . while* (the sense of the passage is
that a courtier needs to change his shirt after playing tennis; Poins, with
only one shirt, has not been seen recently on the tennis-courts)

racket there, as thou hast not done a great while, be-
21   cause the rest of thy low countries have made a shift to
22   eat up thy holland. And God knows whether those that
bawl out the ruins of thy linen shall inherit his kingdom.
But the midwives say the children are not in the fault,
whereupon the world increases, and kindreds are
mightily strengthened.

POINS How ill it follows, after you have labored so hard,
you should talk so idly! Tell me, how many good young
princes would do so, their fathers being so sick as yours
at this time is?

PRINCE Shall I tell thee one thing, Poins?

POINS Yes, faith, and let it be an excellent good thing.

PRINCE It shall serve among wits of no higher breeding
than thine.

34   POINS Go to. I stand the push of your one thing that you
will tell.

PRINCE Marry, I tell thee, it is not meet that I should be
sad, now my father is sick. Albeit I could tell to thee, as
to one it pleases me, for fault of a better, to call my
friend, I could be sad, and sad indeed too.

40   POINS Very hardly upon such a subject.

PRINCE By this hand, thou thinkest me as far in the
42   devil's book as thou and Falstaff for obduracy and
persistency. Let the end try the man. But I tell thee, my
heart bleeds inwardly that my father is so sick. And
keeping such vile company as thou art hath in reason
46   taken from me all ostentation of sorrow.

POINS The reason?

PRINCE What wouldst thou think of me if I should
weep?

---

21 *thy low countries* i.e. the brothels frequented by Poins; *made a shift*
contrived, with a play upon 'shift' meaning shirt   22 *holland* best linen
22–23 *those . . . linen* i.e. your bastards, who wear your shirts   34 *push*
thrust   40 *Very hardly* with great difficulty   42 *obduracy* unregeneracy
46 *ostentation* outward display

POINS I would think thee a most princely hypocrite.

PRINCE It would be every man's thought, and thou art a
blessed fellow to think as every man thinks. Never a
man's thought in the world keeps the roadway better
than thine. Every man would think me an hypocrite
indeed. And what accites your most worshipful thought 55
to think so?

POINS Why, because you have been so lewd and so much 57
engraffed to Falstaff.   58

PRINCE And to thee.

POINS By this light, I am well spoke on; I can hear it with
mine own ears. The worst that they can say of me is that
I am a second brother and that I am a proper fellow of 62
my hands, and those two things I confess I cannot help.
By the mass, here comes Bardolph.

    Enter Bardolph and Boy [Page].

PRINCE And the boy that I gave Falstaff. 'A had him from
me Christian, and look if the fat villain have not transformed him ape.

BARDOLPH God save your grace!

PRINCE And yours, most noble Bardolph!

POINS Come, you virtuous ass, you bashful fool, must
you be blushing? Wherefore blush you now? What a 71
maidenly man-at-arms are you become! Is't such a
matter to get a pottle-pot's maidenhead?   73

PAGE 'A calls me e'en now, my lord, through a red lattice, 74
and I could discern no part of his face from the window.
At last I spied his eyes, and methought he had made two
holes in the ale-wife's new petticoat and so peeped
through.

PRINCE Has not the boy profited?   79

---

55 *accites* arouses 57 *lewd* base 58 *engraffed* attached 62 *second brother*
younger son, without inheritance 62–63 *proper . . . hands* good fighter 71
blushing (Bardolph's red face calls forth this jibe and what follows) 73
get . . . maidenhead drink up a two-quart tankard of ale 74 *red lattice* (the
lattices of the tavern windows were painted red) 79 *profited* become
proficient

BARDOLPH Away, you whoreson upright rabbit, away!

81 PAGE Away, you rascally Althaea's dream, away!

PRINCE Instruct us, boy. What dream, boy?

83 PAGE Marry, my lord, Althaea dreamed she was delivered of a firebrand, and therefore I call him her dream.

PRINCE A crown's worth of good interpretation. There 'tis, boy.

POINS O, that this good blossom could be kept from
88 cankers! Well, there is sixpence to preserve thee.

BARDOLPH An you do not make him hanged among you, the gallows shall have wrong.

PRINCE And how doth thy master, Bardolph?

BARDOLPH Well, my lord. He heard of your grace's coming to town. There's a letter for you.

94 POINS Delivered with good respect. And how doth the
95 martlemas, your master?

BARDOLPH In bodily health, sir.

POINS Marry, the immortal part needs a physician, but that moves not him. Though that be sick, it dies not.

99 PRINCE I do allow this wen to be as familiar with me as my dog, and he holds his place, for look you how he writes.

POINS [reads] 'John Falstaff, knight' – every man must know that, as oft as he has occasion to name himself. Even like those that are kin to the king, for they never prick their finger but they say, 'There's some of the king's blood spilt.' 'How comes that?' says he that takes upon him not to conceive. The answer is as ready as a borrower's cap, 'I am the king's poor cousin, sir.'

---

81 *Althaea's dream* (Althaea dreamed that her son would live only so long as a brand burned in the fire) 83–85 (the page, suffering from a little learning, describes Hecuba's dream, not Althaea's) 88 *cankers* canker worms 94 *good respect* proper ceremony (spoken ironically) 95 *martlemas* martlemas beef, i.e. beef fattened for slaughter on Martinmas Day (November 11) 99 *wen* tumor

PRINCE Nay, they will be kin to us, or they will fetch it   108
from Japhet. But to the letter. *[reads]* 'Sir John Falstaff,
knight, to the son of the king, nearest his father, Harry
Prince of Wales, greeting.'

POINS Why, this is a certificate.   112

PRINCE Peace! *[reads]* 'I will imitate the honorable
Romans in brevity.'

POINS He sure means brevity in breath, short-winded.

[PRINCE *reads*] 'I commend me to thee, I commend thee,
and I leave thee. Be not too familiar with Poins, for he
misuses thy favors so much that he swears thou art to
marry his sister Nell. Repent at idle times as thou
mayest, and so farewell.

'Thine, by yea and no, which is as much as to say, as   121
thou usest him, JACK FALSTAFF with my familiars,
JOHN with my brothers and sisters, and SIR JOHN
with all Europe.'

POINS My lord, I'll steep this letter in sack and make him
eat it.

PRINCE That's to make him eat twenty of his words. But   127
do you use me thus, Ned? Must I marry your sister?

POINS God send the wench no worse fortune! But I never
said so.

PRINCE Well, thus we play the fools with the time, and
the spirits of the wise sit in the clouds and mock us. Is
your master here in London?

BARDOLPH Yea, my lord.

PRINCE Where sups he? Doth the old boar feed in the
old frank?   136

BARDOLPH At the old place, my lord, in Eastcheap.

PRINCE What company?

108–09 *fetch . . . Japhet* trace their ancestry back to Noah's son Japhet
(traditionally regarded as the progenitor of the peoples of Europe)   **112**
certificate legal document   **121** *by yea and no* (a Puritan oath)   **127** *twenty*
(used loosely to mean a large number)   **136** *frank* sty

139 PAGE Ephesians, my lord, of the old church.

PRINCE Sup any women with him?

PAGE None, my lord, but old Mistress Quickly and Mistress Doll Tearsheet.

143 PRINCE What pagan may that be?

PAGE A proper gentlewoman, sir, and a kinswoman of my master's.

PRINCE Even such kin as the parish heifers are to the town bull. Shall we steal upon them, Ned, at supper?

POINS I am your shadow, my lord; I'll follow you.

PRINCE Sirrah, you boy, and Bardolph, no word to your
150 master that I am yet come to town. There's for your silence.

BARDOLPH I have no tongue, sir.

PAGE And for mine, sir, I will govern it.

PRINCE Fare you well; go. *[Exeunt Bardolph and Page.]*
155 This Doll Tearsheet should be some road.

POINS I warrant you, as common as the way between Saint Alban's and London.

158 PRINCE How might we see Falstaff bestow himself to-night in his true colors, and not ourselves be seen?

160 POINS Put on two leathern jerkins and aprons, and wait
161 upon him at his table as drawers.

PRINCE From a God to a bull? A heavy descension! It
163 was Jove's case. From a prince to a prentice? A low transformation! That shall be mine, for in everything
165 the purpose must weigh with the folly. Follow me, Ned.

                                               Exeunt.

*

139 *Ephesians . . . church* i.e. boon companions   143 *pagan* strumpet   150 *There's* there's money   155 *road* i.e. whore (who, like a highway, is common to all)   158 *bestow* behave   160 *jerkins* jackets   161 *drawers* servers of liquor   163 *Jove's case* (for love of Europa, Jove transformed himself into a bull)   165 *weigh with* be equal to

Enter Northumberland, his Wife [Lady
Northumberland], and the Wife to Harry Percy
[Lady Percy].

NORTHUMBERLAND

I pray thee, loving wife, and gentle daughter,   1
Give even way unto my rough affairs.   2
Put not you on the visage of the times
And be like them to Percy troublesome.

LADY NORTHUMBERLAND

I have given over, I will speak no more.
Do what you will, your wisdom be your guide.

NORTHUMBERLAND

Alas, sweet wife, my honor is at pawn,
And, but my going, nothing can redeem it.   8

LADY PERCY

O yet, for God's sake, go not to these wars!
The time was, father, that you broke your word,
When you were more endeared to it than now,   11
When your own Percy, when my heart's dear Harry,   12
Threw many a northward look to see his father
Bring up his powers, but he did long in vain.
Who then persuaded you to stay at home?
There were two honors lost, yours and your son's.
For yours, the God of heaven brighten it!   17
For his, it stuck upon him as the sun
In the grey vault of heaven, and by his light   19
Did all the chivalry of England move
To do brave acts. He was indeed the glass   21
Wherein the noble youth did dress themselves.
[He had no legs that practiced not his gait;
And speaking thick, which nature made his blemish,   24
Became the accents of the valiant,

II, iii Northumberland's castle **1** *daughter* i.e. daughter-in-law **2** *even way* free scope **8** *but* except for **11** *endeared* bound by duty **12–14** *When . . . vain* (a reference to Northumberland's failure to come to his son's support at Shrewsbury) **17** *For* as for **19** *grey* sky-blue **21** *glass* mirror **24** *thick* fast

For those that could speak low and tardily
Would turn their own perfection to abuse,
To seem like him. So that in speech, in gait,
29　In diet, in affections of delight,
30　In military rules, humors of blood,
He was the mark and glass, copy and book,
That fashioned others. And him – O wondrous him!
O miracle of men! – him did you leave,
Second to none, unseconded by you,
To look upon the hideous god of war
36　In disadvantage, to abide a field
Where nothing but the sound of Hotspur's name
38　Did seem defensible. So you left him.
Never, O never, do his ghost the wrong
To hold your honor more precise and nice
With others than with him! Let them alone.
The marshal and the archbishop are strong.
Had my sweet Harry had but half their numbers,
To-day might I, hanging on Hotspur's neck,
45　Have talked of Monmouth's grave.]

NORTHUMBERLAND　　　　　　　　Beshrew your heart,
Fair daughter, you do draw my spirits from me
With new lamenting ancient oversights.
But I must go and meet with danger there,
Or it will seek me in another place
And find me worse provided.

LADY NORTHUMBERLAND　　O, fly to Scotland,
Till that the nobles and the armèd commons
Have of their puissance made a little taste.

LADY PERCY
If they get ground and vantage of the king,
Then join you with them, like a rib of steel,
To make strength stronger. But, for all our loves,
First let them try themselves. So did your son;

29 *affections of delight* pleasures　30 *humors of blood* temperament　36
abide a field fight a battle　38 *defensible* able to defend　45 *Monmouth's*
Prince Hal's; *Beshrew* plague on

He was so suffered. So came I a widow,   57
And never shall have length of life enough
To rain upon remembrance with mine eyes,   59
That it may grow and sprout as high as heaven,
For recordation to my noble husband.   61

NORTHUMBERLAND
Come, come, go in with me. 'Tis with my mind
As with the tide swelled up unto his height,
That makes a still-stand, running neither way.
Fain would I go to meet the archbishop,
But many thousand reasons hold me back.
I will resolve for Scotland. There am I,
Till time and vantage crave my company.   *Exeunt.* 68

*

Enter a Drawer or two [Francis and a second].   II, iv
FRANCIS What the devil hast thou brought there? Apple-   1
    johns? Thou knowest Sir John cannot endure an apple-
    john.
2. DRAWER Mass, thou sayest true. The prince once set a
    dish of apple-johns before him, and told him there were
    five more Sir Johns, and, putting off his hat, said, 'I will
    now take my leave of these six dry, round, old, withered
    knights.' It angered him to the heart. But he hath forgot
    that.
FRANCIS Why, then, cover, and set them down. And see   10
    if thou canst find out Sneak's noise; Mistress Tear-   11
    sheet would fain hear some music. Dispatch. The room
    where they supped is too hot; they'll come in straight.
    Enter Will [a third Drawer].
3. DRAWER Sirrah, here will be the prince and Master

---

57 *suffered* allowed to have his own way   59 *rain* weep   61 *recordation*
memorial   68 *vantage* superiority
II, iv Within an Eastcheap tavern   1-2 *Apple-johns* kind of apple that looks
withered when ripe   10 *cover* lay the cloth   11 *noise* band of musicians

Poins anon, and they will put on two of our jerkins and aprons, and Sir John must not know of it. Bardolph hath brought word. *[Exit.]*

18 FRANCIS By the mass, here will be old Utis. It will be an excellent stratagem.

2. DRAWER I'll see if I can find out Sneak. *Exit.*

Enter Mistress Quickly [the Hostess] and Doll Tearsheet.

HOSTESS I' faith, sweetheart, methinks now you are in an
22 excellent good temperality. Your pulsidge beats as
23 extraordinarily as heart would desire, and your color, I warrant you, is as red as any rose, in good truth, la! But,
25 i' faith, you have drunk too much canaries, and that's a
26 marvellous searching wine, and it perfumes the blood ere one can say, 'What's this?' How do you now?

DOLL Better than I was. Hem!

HOSTESS Why, that's well said. A good heart 's worth gold. Lo, here comes Sir John.

Enter Sir John [Falstaff].

31 FALSTAFF *[sings]* 'When Arthur first in court' – Empty
32 the jordan. *[Exit Francis.]* – *[sings]* 'And was a worthy king.' – How now, Mistress Doll!

34 HOSTESS Sick of a calm, yea, good faith.

35 FALSTAFF So is all her sect. An they be once in a calm, they are sick.

37 DOLL A pox damn you, you muddy rascal, is that all the comfort you give me?

39 FALSTAFF You make fat rascals, Mistress Doll.

DOLL I make them! Gluttony and diseases make them; I make them not.

FALSTAFF If the cook help to make the gluttony, you help to make the diseases, Doll. We catch of you, Doll,

---

18 *old Utis* a noisy row **22** *temperality* i.e. temper; *pulsidge* i.e. pulse **23** *extraordinarily* i.e. ordinarily **25** *canaries* a sweet wine **26** *searching* potent **31** *When . . . court* (a snatch from the ballad *Sir Launcelot du Lake*) **32** *jordan* chamber-pot **34** *calm* i.e. qualm **35** *sect* sex **37** *muddy* dirty **39** *rascals* (a pun on 'rascal' meaning lean deer)

we catch of you. Grant that, my poor virtue, grant that.

DOLL Yea, joy, our chains and our jewels.

FALSTAFF 'Your brooches, pearls, and ouches.' For to 46
serve bravely is to come halting off, you know. To come
off the breach with his pike bent bravely, and to surgery
bravely; to venture upon the charged chambers 49
bravely—

DOLL Hang yourself, you muddy conger, hang yourself! 50

HOSTESS By my troth, this is the old fashion. You two
never meet but you fall to some discord. You are both, i'
good truth, as rheumatic as two dry toasts; you cannot 53
one bear with another's confirmities. What the good- 54
year! One must bear, and that must be you [*to Doll*].
You are the weaker vessel, as they say, the emptier
vessel.

DOLL Can a weak empty vessel bear such a huge full hogs-
head? There's a whole merchant's venture of Bordeaux 58
stuff in him; you have not seen a hulk better stuffed in
the hold. Come, I'll be friends with thee, Jack. Thou art
going to the wars, and whether I shall ever see thee
again or no, there is nobody cares.

    Enter Drawer [Francis].

FRANCIS Sir, Ancient Pistol 's below and would speak 63
with you.

DOLL Hang him, swaggering rascal! Let him not come
hither. It is the foul-mouthed'st rogue in England.

HOSTESS If he swagger, let him not come here. No, by my
faith. I must live among my neighbors, I'll no swaggerers. I am in good name and fame with the very best.
Shut the door, there comes no swaggerers here. I have
not lived all this while to have swaggering now. Shut the
door, I pray you.

---

46 *Your ... ouches* (a snatch from another ballad); *ouches* gems **49** *charged
chambers* small cannon **50** *conger* conger eel **53** *rheumatic* (perhaps she
means 'splenetic'); *dry toasts* (which grate upon each other) **54** *confirmities*
i.e. infirmities **54–55** *What the good-year* what the devil **58–59** *merchant's
... stuff* shipload of Bordeaux wine **63** *Ancient* ensign, lieutenant

FALSTAFF Dost thou hear, hostess?

HOSTESS Pray ye, pacify yourself, Sir John. There comes no swaggerers here.

FALSTAFF Dost thou hear? It is mine ancient.

77 HOSTESS Tilly-fally, Sir John, ne'er tell me. Your ancient swaggerer comes not in my doors. I was before Master
79 Tisick, the debuty, t' other day, and, as he said to me, 'twas no longer ago than Wednesday last, 'I' good faith, neighbor Quickly,' says he – Master Dumbe, our minister, was by then – 'neighbor Quickly,' says he, 'receive those that are civil, for,' said he, 'you are in an ill name.' Now 'a said so, I can tell whereupon. 'For,' says he, 'you are an honest woman, and well thought on; therefore take heed what guests you receive. Receive,' says he,
87 'no swaggering companions.' There comes none here. You would bless you to hear what he said. No, I'll no swaggerers.

90 FALSTAFF He's no swaggerer, hostess; a tame cheater, i' faith; you may stroke him as gently as a puppy grey-
92 hound. He'll not swagger with a Barbary hen, if her feathers turn back in any show of resistance. Call him up, drawer.   [Exit Francis.]

HOSTESS Cheater, call you him? I will bar no honest man my house, nor no cheater. But I do not love swaggering, by my troth; I am the worse when one says swagger. Feel, masters, how I shake, look you, I warrant you.

DOLL So you do, hostess.

HOSTESS Do I? Yea, in very truth, do I, an 'twere an aspen leaf. I cannot abide swaggerers.

Enter Ancient Pistol, [Bardolph,] and Bardolph's Boy [Page].

PISTOL God save you, Sir John!

FALSTAFF Welcome, Ancient Pistol. Here, Pistol, I

---

77 *Tilly-fally* nonsense 79 *debuty* deputy 87 *companions* ruffians 90 *cheater* come-on man in a team of confidence men 92 *Barbary hen* guinea hen

charge you with a cup of sack. Do you discharge upon 102
mine hostess.

PISTOL I will discharge upon her, Sir John, with two
bullets. 105

FALSTAFF She is pistol-proof, sir; you shall hardly offend 106
her.

HOSTESS Come, I'll drink no proofs nor no bullets. I'll
drink no more than will do me good, for no man's
pleasure, I.

PISTOL Then to you, Mistress Dorothy; I will charge you.

DOLL Charge me! I scorn you, scurvy companion. What!
You poor, base, rascally, cheating, lack-linen mate! 111
Away, you mouldy rogue, away! I am meat for your
master.

PISTOL I know you, Mistress Dorothy.

DOLL Away, you cut-purse rascal! You filthy bung, 115
away! By this wine, I'll thrust my knife in your mouldy
chaps, an you play the saucy cuttle with me. Away, you 117
bottle-ale rascal! You basket-hilt stale juggler, you! 118
Since when, I pray you, sir? God's light, with two
points on your shoulder? Much! 120

PISTOL God let me not live but I will murder your ruff
for this.

FALSTAFF No more, Pistol; I would not have you go off
here. Discharge yourself of our company, Pistol.

HOSTESS No, good Captain Pistol, not here, sweet
captain.

DOLL Captain! Thou abominable damned cheater, art
thou not ashamed to be called captain? An captains were

---

102 *charge* toast (with a play on the name Pistol) 102–03 *discharge . . .
hostess* toast the hostess 105 *bullets* (an indecency which the hostess fails
to understand) 106 *offend* wound 111 *mate* (a term of contempt) 115
bung pickpocket 117 *chaps* cheeks; *cuttle* cut-throat 118 *basket-hilt stale
juggler* an impostor who pretends to be a soldier by carrying a sword with a
basketlike hand-guard 120 *points* laces by which pieces of armor were tied
to the shoulders

128 of my mind, they would truncheon you out for taking
their names upon you before you have earned them.
You a captain! You slave, for what? For tearing a poor
whore's ruff in a bawdy-house? He a captain! Hang
him, rogue! He lives upon mouldy stewed prunes and
dried cakes. A captain! God's light, these villains will
134 make the word as odious as the word 'occupy,' which
135 was an excellent good word before it was ill sorted.
Therefore captains had need look to't.

BARDOLPH Pray thee, go down, good ancient.

FALSTAFF Hark thee hither, Mistress Doll.

PISTOL Not I. I tell thee what, Corporal Bardolph, I
could tear her. I'll be revenged of her.

PAGE Pray thee, go down.

142 PISTOL I'll see her damned first, to Pluto's damned lake,
143 by this hand, to the infernal deep, with Erebus and
tortures vile also. Hold hook and line, say I. Down,
145 down, dogs! Down, faitors! Have we not Hiren here?

HOSTESS Good Captain Peesel, be quiet; 'tis very late, i'
147 faith. I beseek you now, aggravate your choler.

PISTOL
These be good humors, indeed! Shall pack-horses
149 And hollow pampered jades of Asia,
Which cannot go but thirty mile a-day,
151 Compare with Caesars, and with Cannibals,
152 And Trojan Greeks? Nay, rather damn them with
153 King Cerberus, and let the welkin roar.
Shall we fall foul for toys?

HOSTESS By my troth, captain, these are very bitter
words.

---

128 *truncheon* beat with a truncheon or staff **134** *occupy* fornicate **135**
ill sorted misused **142** *Pluto's . . . lake* (Pistol confuses the river Styx with a
lake) **143** *Erebus* the underworld **145** *faitors* impostors; *Have . . . here*
(a quotation from a play by George Peele) **147** *aggravate* i.e. moderate
149–50 *And . . . day* (a garbled quotation from Marlowe's *Tamburlaine*,
Part II) **151** *Cannibals* i.e. Hannibals **152** *Trojan Greeks* (Trojans and
Greeks are all one to the excited Pistol) **153** *Cerberus* the three-headed dog
who guarded the entrance to Hades

BARDOLPH Be gone, good ancient. This will grow to a
brawl anon.

PISTOL Die men like dogs! Give crowns like pins! Have
we not Hiren here?

HOSTESS O' my word, captain, there's none such here.
What the good-year! Do you think I would deny her?
For God's sake, be quiet.

PISTOL
Then feed, and be fat, my fair Calipolis.   163
Come, give's some sack.
'Si fortune me tormente, sperato me contento.'   165
Fear we broadsides? No, let the fiend give fire.
Give me some sack. And, sweetheart, lie thou there.
[*Lays down his sword.*]
Come we to full points here, and are etceteras nothing?   168

FALSTAFF Pistol, I would be quiet.

PISTOL Sweet knight, I kiss thy neif. What! We have   170
seen the seven stars.   171

DOLL For God's sake, thrust him down stairs. I cannot
endure such a fustian rascal.   173

PISTOL Thrust him down stairs! Know we not Galloway   174
nags?

FALSTAFF Quoit him down, Bardolph, like a shove-   176
groat shilling. Nay, an 'a do nothing but speak nothing,
'a shall be nothing here.

BARDOLPH Come, get you down stairs.

PISTOL
What! shall we have incision? Shall we imbrue?   180
[*Snatches up his sword.*]
Then death rock me asleep, abridge my doleful days!

---

163 *Then . . . Calipolis* (a burlesque of a line in another play by Peele) 165
Si . . . contento (a multilingual misquotation of a proverb meaning 'If
fortune torments me, hope contents me') 168 *full points* full stops, periods
170 *neif* fist 171 *seven stars* the Pleiades (the idea is that Falstaff and
Pistol have often made a night of it) 173 *fustian* worthless 174–75
Galloway nags Irish horses of inferior breed 176 *Quoit* throw 176–77
shove-groat shilling a coin used in a game somewhat like shuffleboard
played on a smooth table 180 *incision* bloodshed; *imbrue* shed blood

Why, then, let grievous, ghastly, gaping wounds
183 Untwine the Sisters Three! Come, Atropos, I say!

HOSTESS Here's a goodly stuff toward!

FALSTAFF Give me my rapier, boy.

DOLL I pray thee, Jack, I pray thee, do not draw.

FALSTAFF Get you down stairs.
[Draws, and drives Pistol out.]

HOSTESS Here's a goodly tumult! I'll forswear keeping
189 house afore I'll be in these tirrits and frights. So,
murder, I warrant now. Alas, alas! Put up your naked
weapons, put up your naked weapons.
[Exeunt Pistol and Bardolph.]

DOLL I pray thee, Jack, be quiet; the rascal 's gone. Ah,
you whoreson little valiant villain, you!

HOSTESS Are you not hurt i' the groin? Methought 'a
made a shrewd thrust at your belly.
[Enter Bardolph.]

FALSTAFF Have you turned him out o' doors?

BARDOLPH Yea, sir. The rascal 's drunk. You have hurt
him, sir, i' the shoulder.

FALSTAFF A rascal! to brave me!

DOLL Ah, you sweet little rogue, you! Alas, poor ape,
how thou sweatest! Come, let me wipe thy face; come
202 on, you whoreson chops. Ah, rogue! i' faith, I love thee.
Thou art as valorous as Hector of Troy, worth five of
204 Agamemnon, and ten times better than the Nine Worthies. Ah, villain!

FALSTAFF A rascally slave! I will toss the rogue in a
blanket.

DOLL Do, an thou darest for thy heart. An thou dost, I'll
208 canvass thee between a pair of sheets.
Enter Music.

---

183 *Sisters Three* the Fates, of whom Atropos was one   189 *tirrits* fits of
temper   202 *chops* fat-cheeked fellow   204 *Nine Worthies* Hector,
Alexander, Julius Caesar, Joshua, David, Judas Maccabaeus, Arthur,
Charlemagne, Godfrey of Bouillon   208 *canvass* toss in a canvas sheet (but
Doll gives her own special meaning to the expression); s.d. *Music* musicians

PAGE The music is come, sir.

FALSTAFF Let them play. Play, sirs. Sit on my knee, Doll. A rascal bragging slave! The rogue fled from me like quicksilver.

DOLL I' faith, and thou followedst him like a church. Thou whoreson little tidy Bartholomew boar-pig, when 214 wilt thou leave fighting o' days and foining o' nights, 215 and begin to patch up thine old body for heaven?

Enter [behind] Prince [Henry] and Poins [disguised].

FALSTAFF Peace, good Doll! Do not speak like a death's- 217 head. Do not bid me remember mine end.

DOLL Sirrah, what humor 's the prince of?

FALSTAFF A good shallow young fellow. 'A would have made a good pantler, 'a would ha' chipped bread well. 221

DOLL They say Poins has a good wit.

FALSTAFF He a good wit? Hang him, baboon! His wit 's as thick as Tewkesbury mustard. There's no more 224 conceit in him than is in a mallet. 225

DOLL Why does the prince love him so, then?

FALSTAFF Because their legs are both of a bigness, and 'a plays at quoits well, and eats conger and fennel, and 228 drinks off candles' ends for flap-dragons, and rides the 229 wild-mare with the boys, and jumps upon joined-stools, 230 and swears with a good grace, and wears his boots very smooth, like unto the sign of the leg, and breeds no bate 232 with telling of discreet stories; and such other gambol

---

214 *Bartholomew boar-pig* (roast pig was a favorite delicacy at Bartholomew Fair, held annually on August 24 at Smithfield) 215 *foining* thrusting 217–18 *death's-head* (the figure of a skull was used traditionally as a reminder of mortality) 221 *pantler* pantryman; *chipped bread* cut off the crusts 224 *Tewkesbury mustard* (Tewkesbury mustard balls were famous) 225 *conceit* wit 228 *conger and fennel* the meat of conger eel highly seasoned with fennel 229 *drinks . . . flap-dragons* (lighted candles were floated in a glass of liquor, and the trick was either to drink the liquor without disturbing the candle, or, more daringly, to take the candle in the mouth and extinguish the flame by closing the mouth) 230 *wild-mare* seesaw; *joined-stools* stools expertly made by a joiner 232 *sign . . . leg* sign over the door of a bootmaker's shop; *bate* quarrel

faculties 'a has, that show a weak mind and an able body, for the which the prince admits him. For the prince himself is such another; the weight of a hair will turn the scales between their avoirdupois.

238 PRINCE Would not this nave of a wheel have his ears cut off?

POINS Let's beat him before his whore.

240 PRINCE Look, whether the withered elder hath not his poll clawed like a parrot.

POINS Is it not strange that desire should so many years outlive performance?

FALSTAFF Kiss me, Doll.

245 PRINCE Saturn and Venus this year in conjunction! What says the almanac to that?

247 POINS And look whether the fiery Trigon, his man, be
248 not lisping to his master's old tables, his note-book, his counsel-keeper.

250 FALSTAFF Thou dost give me flattering busses.

DOLL By my troth, I kiss thee with a most constant heart.

FALSTAFF I am old, I am old.

DOLL I love thee better than I love e'er a scurvy young boy of them all.

255 FALSTAFF What stuff wilt have a kirtle of? I shall receive money o' Thursday. Shalt have a cap to-morrow. A merry song, come. It grows late; we'll to bed. Thou'lt forget me when I am gone.

DOLL By my troth, thou'lt set me a-weeping, an thou sayest so. Prove that ever I dress myself handsome till
261 thy return. Well, hearken a' th' end.

---

238 *nave* large hub of the wheel of a country cart (with a play upon 'knave')
240–41 *elder . . . parrot* (Doll is rumpling Falstaff's hair)   245 *Saturn* the planet believed to be especially influential upon the aged   247 *fiery Trigon* the three fiery signs of the Zodiac – Aries, Leo, and Sagittarius (alluding to Bardolph's red face)   248 *lisping . . . tables* making love to his master's old note-book, i.e. Mistress Quickly   250 *busses* kisses   255 *kirtle* skirt   261 *hearken a' th' end* i.e. in the end you will have proof of my fidelity

FALSTAFF Some sack, Francis.

PRINCE, POINS Anon, anon, sir.
    [Come forward.]

FALSTAFF Ha! a bastard son of the king's? And art not thou Poins his brother?

PRINCE Why, thou globe of sinful continents, what a life 266 dost thou lead!

FALSTAFF A better than thou. I am a gentleman, thou art a drawer.

PRINCE Very true, sir, and I come to draw you out by the ears.

HOSTESS O, the Lord preserve thy good grace! By my troth, welcome to London. Now, the Lord bless that sweet face of thine! O Jesu, are you come from Wales?

FALSTAFF Thou whoreson mad compound of majesty, 275 by this light flesh and corrupt blood, thou art welcome. 276

DOLL How, you fat fool! I scorn you.

POINS My lord, he will drive you out of your revenge and turn all to a merriment, if you take not the heat. 279

PRINCE You whoreson candle-mine you, how vilely did 280 you speak of me even now before this honest, virtuous, civil gentlewoman!

HOSTESS God's blessing of your good heart! And so she is, by my troth.

FALSTAFF Didst thou hear me?

PRINCE Yea, and you knew me, as you did when you ran 286 away by Gad's Hill. You knew I was at your back, and spoke it on purpose to try my patience.

FALSTAFF No, no, no; not so. I did not think thou wast within hearing.

PRINCE I shall drive you then to confess the willful abuse, and then I know how to handle you.

FALSTAFF No abuse, Hal, o' mine honor, no abuse.

---

266 *continents* (with a play upon 'continence')   275 *compound* lump   276 *light . . . blood* i.e. Doll   279 *if . . . heat* if you do not strike while the iron is hot   280 *candle-mine* mine of tallow   286–87 *as . . . Gad's Hill* (see *1 Henry IV*, II, ii; iv)

PRINCE Not to dispraise me and call me pantler and bread-chipper and I know not what?

FALSTAFF No abuse, Hal.

POINS No abuse?

FALSTAFF No abuse, Ned, i' the world. Honest Ned, none. I dispraised him before the wicked, that the
300 wicked might not fall in love with him. In which doing, I have done the part of a careful friend and a true subject, and thy father is to give me thanks for it. No abuse, Hal. None, Ned, none. No, faith, boys, none.

PRINCE See now, whether pure fear and entire cowardice doth not make thee wrong this virtuous gentlewoman to
306 close with us. Is she of the wicked? Is thine hostess here of the wicked? Or is thy boy of the wicked? Or honest Bardolph, whose zeal burns in his nose, of the wicked?

POINS Answer, thou dead elm, answer.

310 **FALSTAFF** The fiend hath pricked down Bardolph irrecoverable, and his face is Lucifer's privy-kitchen,
312 where he doth nothing but roast malt-worms. For the boy, there is a good angel about him, but the devil blinds him too.

PRINCE For the women?

FALSTAFF For one of them, she is in hell already, and
316 burns poor souls. For the other, I owe her money, and whether she be damned for that, I know not.

HOSTESS No, I warrant you.

319 **FALSTAFF** No, I think thou art not. I think thou art quit for that. Marry, there is another indictment upon thee,
321 for suffering flesh to be eaten in thy house, contrary to the law, for the which I think thou wilt howl.

HOSTESS All victuallers do so. What's a joint of mutton or two in a whole Lent?

PRINCE You, gentlewoman –

---

306 *close* come to terms   310 *pricked down* chosen   312 *malt-worms* topers
316 *burns* infects with venereal disease   319–20 *quit for that* acquitted of
that charge   321–22 *suffering . . . law* permitting meat to be served at your
inn during Lent in defiance of the ordinance which forbade such sale

DOLL What says your grace?

FALSTAFF His grace says that which his flesh rebels
against.

    Peto knocks at door.

HOSTESS Who knocks so loud at door? Look to the door
there, Francis.

    [Enter Peto.]

PRINCE

  Peto, how now! What news?

PETO

  The king your father is at Westminster,
  And there are twenty weak and wearied posts   332
  Come from the north. And as I came along
  I met and overtook a dozen captains,
  Bareheaded, sweating, knocking at the taverns,
  And asking every one for Sir John Falstaff.

PRINCE

  By heaven, Poins, I feel me much to blame,
  So idly to profane the precious time,
  When tempest of commotion, like the south   339
  Borne with black vapor, doth begin to melt   340
  And drop upon our bare unarmèd heads.
  Give me my sword and cloak. Falstaff, good night.

    Exeunt Prince Henry, Poins [, Peto, and Bardolph].

FALSTAFF Now comes in the sweetest morsel of the
night, and we must hence and leave it unpicked.
[Knocking within.] More knocking at the door!

    [Enter Bardolph.]

  How now! What's the matter?

BARDOLPH

  You must away to court, sir, presently.   347
  A dozen captains stay at door for you.

FALSTAFF *[to the Page]* Pay the musicians, sirrah. Farewell, hostess. Farewell, Doll. You see, my good

---

332 *posts* messengers **339** *commotion* insurrection; *south* south wind **340**
Borne laden **347** *presently* immediately

wenches, how men of merit are sought after. The un-
deserver may sleep when the man of action is called on.

353 Farewell, good wenches. If I be not sent away post, I
will see you again ere I go.

DOLL I cannot speak. If my heart be not ready to burst –
well, sweet Jack, have a care of thyself.

FALSTAFF Farewell, farewell.

[Exeunt Falstaff and Bardolph.]

HOSTESS Well, fare thee well. I have known thee these
359 twenty-nine years, come peascod-time, but an honester
and truer-hearted man – well, fare thee well.

BARDOLPH [within] Mistress Tearsheet!

HOSTESS What's the matter?

BARDOLPH [within] Bid Mistress Tearsheet come to my
master.

HOSTESS O, run, Doll, run. Run, good Doll. Come. [to
366 Bardolph within] She comes blubbered. Yea, will you
come, Doll? Exeunt.

*

III, i   Enter the King in his nightgown, alone [with a Page].

KING

Go call the Earls of Surrey and of Warwick.
But, ere they come, bid them o'erread these letters
And well consider of them. Make good speed.

[Exit Page.]

How many thousand of my poorest subjects
Are at this hour asleep! O sleep, O gentle sleep,
Nature's soft nurse, how have I frighted thee,
That thou no more wilt weigh my eyelids down
8 And steep my senses in forgetfulness?
9 Why rather, sleep, liest thou in smoky cribs,

353 *post* posthaste   359 *peascod-time* early summer, when the peas are in
blossom   366 *blubbered* weeping
III, i King Henry's palace (Westminster)   s.d. *nightgown* dressing gown
8 *steep* saturate   9 *cribs* hovels

Upon uneasy pallets stretching thee 10
And hushed with buzzing night-flies to thy slumber,
Than in the perfumed chambers of the great,
Under the canopies of costly state, 13
And lulled with sound of sweetest melody?
O thou dull god, why liest thou with the vile 15
In loathsome beds, and leavest the kingly couch
A watch-case or a common 'larum-bell? 17
Wilt thou upon the high and giddy mast
Seal up the ship-boy's eyes, and rock his brains
In cradle of the rude imperious surge
And in the visitation of the winds,
Who take the ruffian billows by the top,
Curling their monstrous heads and hanging them
With deafening clamor in the slippery clouds,
That, with the hurly, death itself awakes? 25
Canst thou, O partial sleep, give thy repose
To the wet sea-son in an hour so rude,
And in the calmest and most stillest night,
With all appliances and means to boot, 29
Deny it to a king? Then happy low, lie down! 30
Uneasy lies the head that wears a crown.
    Enter Warwick, Surrey, and Sir John Blunt.

WARWICK
    Many good morrows to your majesty!

KING
    Is it good morrow, lords?

WARWICK
    'Tis one o'clock, and past.

KING
    Why, then, good morrow to you all, my lords.
    Have you read o'er the letters that I sent you?

---

10 *uneasy pallets* uncomfortable beds   13 *canopies . . . state* elaborate
canopies over the beds of the wealthy   15 *dull god* Morpheus   17 *watch-
case* sentry-box; *'larum-bell* alarm bell   25 *hurly* tumult   29 *to boot* in
addition   30 *low* lowly folk

79

WARWICK

We have, my liege.

KING

Then you perceive the body of our kingdom
39   How foul it is, what rank diseases grow,
And with what danger, near the heart of it.

WARWICK

41   It is but as a body yet distempered,
Which to his former strength may be restored
With good advice and little medicine.
My Lord Northumberland will soon be cooled.

KING

O God! that one might read the book of fate,
And see the revolution of the times
47   Make mountains level, and the continent,
Weary of solid firmness, melt itself
Into the sea! And other times to see
The beachy girdle of the ocean
Too wide for Neptune's hips, how chances mock,
And changes fill the cup of alteration
With divers liquors! O, if this were seen,
The happiest youth, viewing his progress through,
55   What perils past, what crosses to ensue,
Would shut the book, and sit him down and die.
'Tis not ten years gone
Since Richard and Northumberland, great friends,
Did feast together, and in two years after
Were they at wars. It is but eight years since
This Percy was the man nearest my soul,
Who like a brother toiled in my affairs
63   And laid his love and life under my foot,
Yea, for my sake, even to the eyes of Richard
Gave him defiance. But which of you was by—

---

39 *rank* festering   **41** *distempered* sick   **47** *continent* dry land   **55** *crosses*
troubles   **63** *under my foot* at my disposal

[*To Warwick*]
You, cousin Nevil, as I may remember –   66
When Richard, with his eye brimful of tears,
Then checked and rated by Northumberland,   68
Did speak these words, now proved a prophecy?
'Northumberland, thou ladder by the which   70
My cousin Bolingbroke ascends my throne' –
Though then, God knows, I had no such intent,
But that necessity so bowed the state
That I and greatness were compelled to kiss –
'The time shall come,' thus did he follow it,
'The time will come that foul sin, gathering head,   76
Shall break into corruption.' So went on,
Foretelling this same time's condition
And the division of our amity.

WARWICK
There is a history in all men's lives,
Figuring the nature of the times deceased,   81
The which observed, a man may prophesy,
With a near aim, of the main chance of things   83
As yet not come to life, which in their seeds
And weak beginnings lie intreasurèd.   85
Such things become the hatch and brood of time,
And by the necessary form of this   87
King Richard might create a perfect guess
That great Northumberland, then false to him,
Would of that seed grow to a greater falseness,
Which should not find a ground to root upon,
Unless on you.
KING   Are these things then necessities?

---

66 *Nevil* (actually the family name of the Earl of Warwick at this period was not Nevil but Beauchamps) 68 *rated* berated 70–77 (the lines in quotation marks are paraphrased from *Richard II*, V, i, 55–68) 76 *gathering head* coming to a head 81 *Figuring* revealing 83 *main chance* general probability 85 *intreasurèd* stored up 87 *necessary . . . this* logical application of this principle

Then let us meet them like necessities.
And that same word even now cries out on us.
They say the bishop and Northumberland
Are fifty thousand strong.

WARWICK   It cannot be, my lord.
Rumor doth double, like the voice and echo,
The numbers of the feared. Please it your grace
To go to bed. Upon my soul, my lord,
The powers that you already have sent forth
Shall bring this prize in very easily.
To comfort you the more, I have received
103   A certain instance that Glendower is dead.
Your majesty hath been this fortnight ill,
105   And these unseasoned hours perforce must add
Unto your sickness.

KING   I will take your counsel.
107   And were these inward wars once out of hand,
We would, dear lords, unto the Holy Land.   *Exeunt.*

*

III, ii   *Enter Justice Shallow and Justice Silence [with
Mouldy, Shadow, Wart, Feeble, Bullcalf].*

SHALLOW Come on, come on, come on, sir. Give me your
hand, sir, give me your hand, sir; an early stirrer, by the
3   rood! And how doth my good cousin Silence?

SILENCE Good morrow, good cousin Shallow.

SHALLOW And how doth my cousin, your bedfellow?
And your fairest daughter and mine, my god-daughter
Ellen?

7 SILENCE Alas, a black ousel, cousin Shallow!

SHALLOW By yea and no, sir, I dare say my cousin
William is become a good scholar. He is at Oxford still,

103 *instance* proof   105 *unseasoned* unseasonable   107 *inward* civil; *out of
hand* done with
III, ii Before Shallow's house in Gloucestershire   3 *rood* cross   7 *ousel*
blackbird

is he not?

SILENCE Indeed, sir, to my cost.

SHALLOW 'A must, then, to the Inns o' Court shortly. I 11
was once of Clement's Inn, where I think they will talk 12
of mad Shallow yet.

SILENCE You were called 'lusty Shallow' then, cousin.

SHALLOW By the mass, I was called anything. And I
would have done anything indeed too, and roundly too. 16
There was I, and little John Doit of Staffordshire, and
black George Barnes, and Francis Pickbone, and Will
Squele, a Cotswold man; you had not four such swinge- 19
bucklers in all the Inns o' Court again. And I may say to
you we knew where the bona-robas were and had the 21
best of them all at commandment. Then was Jack Fal- 22
staff, now Sir John, a boy, and page to Thomas Mowbray, Duke of Norfolk.

SILENCE This Sir John, cousin, that comes hither anon
about soldiers?

SHALLOW The same Sir John, the very same. I see him
break Skogan's head at the court-gate, when 'a was a
crack not thus high. And the very same day did I fight 29
with one Sampson Stockfish, a fruiterer, behind Gray's 30
Inn. Jesu, Jesu, the mad days that I have spent! And to
see how many of my old acquaintance are dead!

SILENCE We shall all follow, cousin.

SHALLOW Certain, 'tis certain, very sure, very sure.
Death, as the Psalmist saith, is certain to all, all shall die.
How a good yoke of bullocks at Stamford fair?   36

SILENCE By my troth, I was not there.

SHALLOW Death is certain. Is old Double of your town
living yet?

---

11 *Inns o' Court* the law schools 12 *Clement's Inn* one of the Inns of
Chancery, which in Shallow's time were preparatory to the Inns of Court
16 *roundly* thoroughly 19 *Cotswold* (the Cotswolds are a range of hills in
Gloucestershire); *swinge-bucklers* swashbucklers 21 *bona-robas* wenches
22 *at commandment* at will 29 *crack* lively boy 30–31 *Gray's Inn* one of
the Inns of Court 36 *How* how much

SILENCE Dead, sir.

SHALLOW Jesu, Jesu, dead! 'A drew a good bow, and
42   dead! 'A shot a fine shoot. John a Gaunt loved him well
and betted much money on his head. Dead! 'A would
44   have clapped i' the clout at twelve score, and carried
you a forehand shaft a fourteen and fourteen and a half,
that it would have done a man's heart good to see. How
a score of ewes now?

48 SILENCE Thereafter as they be. A score of good ewes
may be worth ten pounds.

SHALLOW And is old Double dead?

SILENCE Here come two of Sir John Falstaff's men, as I
think.

Enter Bardolph and one with him.

[SHALLOW] Good morrow, honest gentlemen.

BARDOLPH I beseech you, which is Justice Shallow?

54 SHALLOW I am Robert Shallow, sir, a poor esquire of
this county, and one of the king's justices of the peace.
What is your good pleasure with me?

BARDOLPH My captain, sir, commends him to you, my
58   captain, Sir John Falstaff, a tall gentleman, by heaven,
and a most gallant leader.

SHALLOW He greets me well, sir. I knew him a good
61   backsword man. How doth the good knight? May I ask
how my lady his wife doth?

63 BARDOLPH Sir, pardon, a soldier is better accommodated than with a wife.

SHALLOW It is well said, in faith, sir, and it is well said
indeed too. Better accommodated! It is good, yea, indeed, is it. Good phrases are surely, and ever were, very

---

42 *shot . . . shoot* (referring to archery); *John a Gaunt* father of Henry IV
44 *clapped . . . score* hit the mark at 240 yards   44–45 *carried . . . half* could
shoot a heavy arrow point blank (rather than in a curved trajectory) so that
it carried 280 or 290 yards   48 *Thereafter . . . be* the price varies according
to the quality   54 *esquire* gentleman, just below the rank of knight   58
tall valiant   61 *backsword* stick with a basket hilt used instead of a sword
in fencing   63 *accommodated* provided (in Shakespeare's time the word
was considered 'precious')

commendable. Accommodated! It comes of 'accommodo.' Very good, a good phrase.

BARDOLPH Pardon me, sir. I have heard the word. Phrase call you it? By this good day, I know not the phrase, but I will maintain the word with my sword to be a soldierlike word, and a word of exceeding good command, by heaven. Accommodated, that is, when a man is, as they say, accommodated; or when a man is, being, whereby 'a may be thought to be accommodated, which is an excellent thing.

    Enter Sir John Falstaff.

SHALLOW It is very just. Look, here comes good Sir 78 John. Give me your good hand, give me your worship's good hand. By my troth, you like well and bear your 80 years very well. Welcome, good Sir John.

FALSTAFF I am glad to see you well, good Master Robert Shallow. Master Surecard, as I think?

SHALLOW No, Sir John, it is my cousin Silence, in com- 84 mission with me.

FALSTAFF Good Master Silence, it well befits you should be of the peace.

SILENCE Your good worship is welcome.

FALSTAFF Fie! This is hot weather, gentlemen. Have you provided me here half a dozen sufficient men?   90

SHALLOW Marry, have we, sir. Will you sit?

FALSTAFF Let me see them, I beseech you.

SHALLOW Where's the roll? Where's the roll? Where's the roll? Let me see, let me see, let me see. So, so, so, so, 94 so, so, so. Yea, marry, sir. Ralph Mouldy! Let them appear as I call, let them do so, let them do so. Let me see, where is Mouldy?

MOULDY Here, an't please you.

SHALLOW What think you, Sir John? A good-limbed

---

78 *It . . . just* that's very true   80 *like* thrive   84–85 *in . . . me* we both hold commissions as justices of the peace   90 *sufficient* able   94–95 *So . . . so* (Shallow goes through the business of checking the men against the names on the muster roll)

100   fellow, young, strong, and of good friends.

FALSTAFF Is thy name Mouldy?

MOULDY Yea, an't please you.

FALSTAFF 'Tis the more time thou wert used.

SHALLOW Ha, ha, ha! most excellent, i' faith! Things
that are mouldy lack use. Very singular good! In faith,
well said, Sir John, very well said.

107 [FALSTAFF Prick him.]

MOULDY I was pricked well enough before, an you could
109   have let me alone. My old dame will be undone now for
110   one to do her husbandry and her drudgery. You need not
to have pricked me. There are other men fitter to go out
than I.

FALSTAFF Go to. Peace, Mouldy, you shall go. Mouldy,
it is time you were spent.

MOULDY Spent!

SHALLOW Peace, fellow, peace. Stand aside. Know you
where you are? For the other, Sir John, let me see.
Simon Shadow!

FALSTAFF Yea, marry, let me have him to sit under. He's
120   like to be a cold soldier.

SHALLOW Where's Shadow?

SHADOW Here, sir.

FALSTAFF Shadow, whose son art thou?

SHADOW My mother's son, sir.

FALSTAFF Thy mother's son! Like enough, and thy
father's shadow. So the son of the female is the shadow
of the male. It is often so, indeed, but much of the
father's substance!

SHALLOW Do you like him, Sir John?

FALSTAFF Shadow will serve for summer. Prick him, for
131   we have a number of shadows to fill up the muster-book.

SHALLOW Thomas Wart!

FALSTAFF Where's he?

---

100 *friends* family   **107** *Prick* choose   **109** *dame* mother   **110** *husbandry*
farm work   **131** *shadows* names of non-existent men for whom the commanding officer received pay

WART Here, sir.

FALSTAFF Is thy name Wart?

WART Yea, sir.

FALSTAFF Thou art a very ragged wart.

SHALLOW Shall I prick him down, Sir John?

FALSTAFF It were superfluous, for his apparel is built
upon his back and the whole frame stands upon pins. 140
Prick him no more.

SHALLOW Ha, ha, ha! you can do it, sir, you can do it. I 142
commend you well. Francis Feeble!

FEEBLE Here, sir.

SHALLOW What trade art thou, Feeble?

FEEBLE A woman's tailor, sir.

SHALLOW Shall I prick him, sir?

FALSTAFF You may. But if he had been a man's tailor,
he'd a' pricked you. Wilt thou make as many holes in an 149
enemy's battle as thou hast done in a woman's petticoat? 150

FEEBLE I will do my good will, sir. You can have no more.

FALSTAFF Well said, good woman's tailor! Well said,
courageous Feeble! Thou wilt be as valiant as the
wrathful dove or most magnanimous mouse. Prick the 154
woman's tailor well, Master Shallow, deep, Master
Shallow.

FEEBLE I would Wart might have gone, sir.

FALSTAFF I would thou wert a man's tailor, that thou
mightst mend him and make him fit to go. I cannot put
him to a private soldier that is the leader of so many
thousands. Let that suffice, most forcible Feeble. 159

FEEBLE It shall suffice, sir.

FALSTAFF I am bound to thee, reverend Feeble. Who is
next?

SHALLOW Peter Bullcalf o' the green!

FALSTAFF Yea, marry, let's see Bullcalf.

BULLCALF Here, sir.

---

140 *stands* depends   **142** *you . . . it* you know how to do it   **149** *pricked*
attired   **150** *battle* army   **154** *magnanimous* stout-hearted   **159** *thousands*
i.e. of lice

FALSTAFF 'Fore God, a likely fellow! Come, prick Bullcalf till he roar again.

BULLCALF O Lord! good my lord captain –

FALSTAFF What, dost thou roar before thou art pricked?

BULLCALF O Lord, sir! I am a diseased man.

FALSTAFF What disease hast thou?

BULLCALF A whoreson cold, sir, a cough, sir, which I
173   caught with ringing in the king's affairs upon his coronation day, sir.

175 FALSTAFF Come, thou shalt go to the wars in a gown. We
will have away thy cold, and I will take such order that
thy friends shall ring for thee. Is here all?

SHALLOW Here is two more called than your number.
You must have but four here, sir. And so, I pray you, go
in with me to dinner.

FALSTAFF Come, I will go drink with you, but I cannot
182   tarry dinner. I am glad to see you, by my troth, Master
Shallow.

184 SHALLOW O, Sir John, do you remember since we lay all
185   night in the Windmill in Saint George's Field?

FALSTAFF No more of that, good Master Shallow, no
more of that.

SHALLOW Ha! 'Twas a merry night. And is Jane Nightwork alive?

FALSTAFF She lives, Master Shallow.

190 SHALLOW She never could away with me.

FALSTAFF Never, never, she would always say she could
not abide Master Shallow.

SHALLOW By the mass, I could anger her to the heart.
She was then a bona-roba. Doth she hold her own well?

FALSTAFF Old, old, Master Shallow.

SHALLOW Nay, she must be old. She cannot choose but

173–74 *ringing ... day* ringing church bells in celebration of the anniversary
of the king's coronation   175 *gown* dressing gown   182 *tarry* stay for   184
since when   185 *Windmill* a brothel; *Saint George's Field* a favorite Sunday
resort of Londoners, on the Surrey side of the Thames   190 *away with*
tolerate

be old. Certain she's old, and had Robin Nightwork by
old Nightwork before I came to Clement's Inn.

SILENCE That's fifty-five year ago.

SHALLOW Ha, cousin Silence, that thou hadst seen that
that this knight and I have seen! Ha, Sir John, said I
well?

FALSTAFF We have heard the chimes at midnight, Master
Shallow.

SHALLOW That we have, that we have, that we have, in
faith, Sir John, we have. Our watchword was 'Hem,   205
boys!' Come, let's to dinner, come, let's to dinner.
Jesus, the days that we have seen! Come, come.

                    Exeunt [Falstaff and the Justices].

BULLCALF Good Master Corporate Bardolph, stand my   208
friend, and here's four Harry ten shillings in French   209
crowns for you. In very truth, sir, I had as lief be hanged,
sir, as go. And yet for mine own part, sir, I do not care,
but rather, because I am unwilling, and, for mine own
part, have a desire to stay with my friends. Else, sir, I
did not care, for mine own part, so much.

BARDOLPH Go to, stand aside.

MOULDY And, good master corporal captain, for my old
dame's sake, stand my friend. She has nobody to do anything about her when I am gone, and she is old, and cannot help herself. You shall have forty, sir.   219

BARDOLPH Go to, stand aside.

FEEBLE By my troth, I care not. A man can die but once.
We owe God a death. I'll ne'er bear a base mind. An't be   222
my destiny, so. An't be not, so. No man is too good to
serve's prince. And let it go which way it will, he that
dies this year is quit for the next.   225

205–06 *Hem, boys!* here's how! down the hatch!   208 *Corporate* i.e.
corporal   209–10 *four ... crowns* (an anachronism; the 'Harry ten shilling'
piece was first coined in the reign of Henry VII. In Shakespeare's time one
of these pieces was worth 5s.; a French crown was worth 4s. Bullcalf's
'present' was five French crowns, the equivalent of one pound.)   219 *forty*
probably forty shillings, or two pounds   222 *bear* harbor   225 *quit* free

BARDOLPH Well said. Th' art a good fellow.

FEEBLE Faith, I'll bear no base mind.

Enter Falstaff and the Justices.

FALSTAFF Come, sir, which men shall I have?

SHALLOW Four of which you please.

BARDOLPH Sir, a word with you. I have three pound to free Mouldy and Bullcalf.

FALSTAFF Go to, well.

SHALLOW Come, Sir John, which four will you have?

FALSTAFF Do you choose for me.

SHALLOW Marry, then, Mouldy, Bullcalf, Feeble, and Shadow.

FALSTAFF Mouldy and Bullcalf. For you, Mouldy, stay at home till you are past service. And for your part, Bullcalf, grow till you come unto it. I will none of you.

SHALLOW Sir John, Sir John, do not yourself wrong. They are your likeliest men, and I would have you served with the best.

FALSTAFF Will you tell me, Master Shallow, how to choose a man? Care I for the limb, the thews, the stature, bulk, and big assemblance of a man! Give me the spirit, Master Shallow. Here's Wart. You see what a ragged appearance it is. 'A shall charge you and discharge you with the motion of a pewterer's hammer, come off and on swifter than he that gibbets on the brewer's bucket. And this same half-faced fellow, Shadow. Give me this man. He presents no mark to the enemy; the foeman may with as great aim level at the edge of a penknife. And for a retreat, how swiftly will this Feeble the woman's tailor run off! O, give me the spare men, and spare me the great ones. Put me a caliver into Wart's hand, Bardolph.

BARDOLPH Hold, Wart, traverse. Thus, thus, thus.

FALSTAFF Come, manage me your caliver. So. Very well.

---

244 *thews* strength   **245** *assemblance* appearance   **247** *charge . . . discharge you* load and fire   **248** *motion . . . hammer* i.e. swift, regular beat   **249** *gibbets . . . bucket* hangs the pails of brew on the yoke of the carrier   **255** *caliver* light musket   **256** *traverse* take aim

Go to. Very good, exceeding good. O, give me always a
little, lean, old, chopped, bald shot. Well said, i' faith, 259
Wart. Th' art a good scab. Hold, there's a tester for thee. 260

SHALLOW He is not his craft's master, he doth not do it
right. I remember at Mile-end Green, when I lay at 262
Clement's Inn – I was then Sir Dagonet in Arthur's show 263
– there was a little quiver fellow, and 'a would manage 264
you his piece thus, and 'a would about and about, and
come you in and come you in. 'Rah, tah, tah,' would 'a
say, 'Bounce,' would 'a say, and away again would 'a go,
and again would 'a come. I shall ne'er see such a fellow.

FALSTAFF These fellows will do well, Master Shallow.
God keep you, Master Silence. I will not use many
words with you. Fare you well, gentlemen both. I thank
you. I must a dozen mile to-night. Bardolph, give the
soldiers coats.

SHALLOW Sir John, the Lord bless you! God prosper
your affairs! God send us peace! At your return visit our
house, let our old acquaintance be renewed. Peradven-
ture I will with ye to the court.

FALSTAFF 'Fore God, would you would, Master Shallow.

SHALLOW Go to, I have spoke at a word. God keep you. 278

FALSTAFF Fare you well, gentle gentlemen. *Exeunt [Jus-
tices].* On, Bardolph, lead the men away. *[Exeunt all but
Falstaff.]* As I return, I will fetch off these justices. I do 281
see the bottom of Justice Shallow. Lord, Lord, how subject we old men are to this vice of lying! This same starved
justice hath done nothing but prate to me of the wildness
of his youth and the feats he hath done about Turnbull 285
Street, and every third word a lie, duer paid to the hearer 286

---

259 *chopped* cnapped; *shot* armed soldier   **260** *scab* a pun on the name
'Wart'; *tester* sixpence   **262** *Mile-end Green* a training ground for citizen
soldiers   **263** *Sir Dagonet* King Arthur's fool; *Arthur's show* a group who
staged an annual archery exhibition, each member taking the name of a
character from Arthurian legend   **264** *quiver* nimble   **278** *at a word*
hastily   **281** *fetch off* get the better of   **285–86** *Turnbull Street* a resort of
prostitutes   **286** *duer* more promptly

287   than the Turk's tribute. I do remember him at Clement's
      Inn like a man made after supper of a cheese-paring.
      When 'a was naked, he was, for all the world, like a forked
      radish, with a head fantastically carved upon it with a
291   knife. 'A was so forlorn that his dimensions to any thick
292   sight were invincible. 'A was the very genius of famine,
      yet lecherous as a monkey, and the whores called him
294   mandrake. 'A came ever in the rearward of the fashion,
295   and sung those tunes to the overscutched huswives that
296   he heard the carmen whistle, and sware they were his
297   fancies or his good-nights. And now is this Vice's dagger
      become a squire, and talks as familiarly of John a Gaunt
      as if he had been sworn brother to him, and I'll be sworn
      'a ne'er saw him but once in the Tilt-yard, and then he
      burst his head for crowding among the marshal's men. I
      saw it, and told John a Gaunt he beat his own name, for
      you might have thrust him and all his apparel into an
304   eel-skin, the case of a treble hautboy was a mansion for
      him, a court. And now has he land and beefs. Well, I'll
      be acquainted with him, if I return, and 't shall go hard
307   but I will make him a philosopher's two stones to me. If
308   the young dace be a bait for the old pike, I see no reason
      in the law of nature but I may snap at him. Let time
      shape, and there an end.   *Exit.*

*

287 *Turk's tribute* tribute-money exacted by the Turk   291 *thick* dull   292
invincible i.e. invisible   294 *mandrake* (the mandrake root resembles the
figure of a man)   295 *overscutched huswives* worn-out hussies   296 *carmen*
wagoners   297 *fancies* musical compositions; *good-nights* good-night
songs; *Vice's dagger* thin wooden dagger carried by Vice, the comic character in the old morality plays   304 *hautboy* oboe   307 *philosopher's two
stones* i.e. the elixir of life (which was believed to preserve health) and the
philosopher's stone (which, it was believed, could transmute base metal into
gold). Both were referred to as stones, although the *'elixir vitae'* was also
regarded as a liquid   308 *dace* small fish used as live bait

Enter the Archbishop [of York], Mowbray, Hastings IV, i
[and others], within the Forest of Gaultree.

ARCHBISHOP
What is this forest called?

HASTINGS
'Tis Gaultree Forest, an't shall please your grace.

ARCHBISHOP
Here stand, my lords, and send discoverers forth   3
To know the numbers of our enemies.

HASTINGS
We have sent forth already.

ARCHBISHOP   'Tis well done.
My friends and brethren in these great affairs,
I must acquaint you that I have received
New-dated letters from Northumberland,
Their cold intent, tenor, and substance, thus:
Here doth he wish his person, with such powers   10
As might hold sortance with his quality,   11
The which he could not levy. Whereupon
He is retired, to ripe his growing fortunes,   13
To Scotland, and concludes in hearty prayers
That your attempts may overlive the hazard   15
And fearful meeting of their opposite.   16

MOWBRAY
Thus do the hopes we have in him touch ground
And dash themselves to pieces.
        Enter a Messenger.

HASTINGS   Now, what news?

MESSENGER
West of this forest, scarcely off a mile,
In goodly form comes on the enemy,   20
And, by the ground they hide, I judge their number
Upon or near the rate of thirty thousand.   22

IV, i Within the forest of Gaultree s.d. *Forest of Gaultree* a royal forest in
Yorkshire 3 *discoverers* scouts 10 *powers* forces 11 *hold sortance* accord;
quality rank 13 *ripe* make ripe 15 *overlive* outlive 16 *opposite* adversary
20 *form* formation 22 *rate* estimated number

MOWBRAY

23   The just proportion that we gave them out.

24   Let us sway on and face them in the field.

ARCHBISHOP

25   What well-appointed leader fronts us here?

Enter Westmoreland.

MOWBRAY

I think it is my Lord of Westmoreland.

WESTMORELAND

Health and fair greeting from our general,

The prince, Lord John and Duke of Lancaster.

ARCHBISHOP

Say on, my Lord of Westmoreland, in peace.

What doth concern your coming?

WESTMORELAND   Then, my lord,

31   Unto your grace do I in chief address

The substance of my speech. If that rebellion

33   Came like itself, in base and abject routs,

34   Led on by bloody youth, guarded with rags,

35   And countenanced by boys and beggary,

36   I say, if damned commotion so appeared,

In his true, native and most proper shape,

You, reverend father, and these noble lords

Had not been here, to dress the ugly form

Of base and bloody insurrection

With your fair honors. You, lord archbishop,

42   Whose see is by a civil peace maintained,

Whose beard the silver hand of peace hath touched,

44   Whose learning and good letters peace hath tutored,

45   Whose white investments figure innocence,

The dove and very blessèd spirit of peace,

47   Wherefore do you so ill translate yourself

---

23 *just . . . out* exact number we estimated   24 *sway* move   25 *well-appointed* well-armed; *fronts* faces   31 *in chief* principally   33 *routs* mobs   34 *guarded* trimmed   35 *countenanced* supported; *beggary* beggars   36 *commotion* rebellion   42 *see* diocese   44 *good letters* study of correct authors   45 *investments* vestments   47 *translate* transform

Out of the speech of peace that bears such grace,
Into the harsh and boisterous tongue of war,
Turning your books to graves, your ink to blood,
Your pens to lances, and your tongue divine
To a loud trumpet and a point of war ?   52

ARCHBISHOP
Wherefore do I this ? So the question stands.
Briefly to this end : we are all diseased,
[And with our surfeiting and wanton hours   55
Have brought ourselves into a burning fever,
And we must bleed for it. Of which disease   57
Our late king, Richard, being infected, died.
But, my most noble Lord of Westmoreland,
I take not on me here as a physician,   60
Nor do I as an enemy to peace
Troop in the throngs of military men,
But rather show awhile like fearful war,
To diet rank minds sick of happiness   64
And purge the obstructions which begin to stop
Our very veins of life. Hear me more plainly.
I have in equal balance justly weighed   67
What wrongs our arms may do, what wrongs we suffer,
And find our griefs heavier than our offenses.   69
We see which way the stream of time doth run,
And are enforced from our most quiet there
By the rough torrent of occasion,   72
And have the summary of all our griefs,
When time shall serve, to show in articles ;   74
Which long ere this we offered to the king,
And might by no suit gain our audience.
When we are wronged and would unfold our griefs,
We are denied access unto his person
Even by those men that most have done us wrong.]

52 *point of war* signal on the trumpet   55 *surfeiting* gluttony; *wanton* self-
indulgent   57 *bleed* be bled, as a therapeutic measure   60 *take ... as* do not
assume the character of   64 *rank* obese   67 *equal* exact   69 *griefs* grievances   72 *occasion* circumstances   74 *articles* an itemized list

  The dangers of the days but newly gone,
  Whose memory is written on the earth
  With yet appearing blood, and the examples
83 Of every minute's instance, present now,
  Hath put us in these ill-beseeming arms,
  Not to break peace or any branch of it,
  But to establish here a peace indeed,
87 Concurring both in name and quality.

WESTMORELAND
  When ever yet was your appeal denied?
89 Wherein have you been gallèd by the king?
90 What peer hath been suborned to grate on you,
  That you should seal this lawless bloody book
  Of forged rebellion with a seal divine
  And consecrate commotion's bitter edge?

ARCHBISHOP
94 My brother general, the commonwealth,
95 To brother born an household cruelty,
  I make my quarrel in particular.

WESTMORELAND
  There is no need of any such redress,
  Or if there were, it not belongs to you.

MOWBRAY
  Why not to him in part, and to us all
  That feel the bruises of the days before,
  And suffer the condition of these times
102 To lay a heavy and unequal hand
  Upon our honors?

WESTMORELAND [O, my good Lord Mowbray,
104 Construe the times to their necessities,

---

83 *Of . . . instance* occurring every minute 87 *Concurring . . . quality* which shall be peace in both name and fact 89 *gallèd* made sore 90 *suborned* bribed; *grate on* vex 94 *brother general* my brothers the people at large 95 (This line has never been explained satisfactorily. It was dropped from the folio, and, along with line 93, from some copies of the quarto. Without it, the archbishop's words are perfectly intelligible.) 102 *unequal* unjust 104 *to* according to

And you shall say indeed, it is the time,
And not the king, that doth you injuries.
Yet for your part, it not appears to me
Either from the king or in the present time
That you should have an inch of any ground
To build a grief on. Were you not restored
To all the Duke of Norfolk's signories,   111
Your noble and right well remembered father's?

MOWBRAY

What thing, in honor, had my father lost,   113
That need to be revived and breathed in me?
The king that loved him, as the state stood then,
Was force perforce compelled to banish him.   116
And then that Henry Bolingbroke and he,
Being mounted and both rousèd in their seats,
Their neighing coursers daring of the spur,
Their armèd staves in charge, their beavers down,   120
Their eyes of fire sparkling through sights of steel,
And the loud trumpet blowing them together,
Then, then, when there was nothing could have stayed
My father from the breast of Bolingbroke,
O, when the king did throw his warder down,   125
His own life hung upon the staff he threw.
Then threw he down himself and all their lives
That by indictment and by dint of sword
Have since miscarried under Bolingbroke.   129

WESTMORELAND

You speak, Lord Mowbray, now you know not what.
The Earl of Hereford was reputed then   131
In England the most valiant gentleman.
Who knows on whom fortune would then have smiled?
But if your father had been victor there,

---

111 *signories* properties **113–29** (for the quarrel between Mowbray and
Bolingbroke see *Richard II*, I, i; iii) **116** *force perforce* whether he wished
it or not **120** *staves in charge* lances ready for action; *beavers* visors of their
helmets **125** *warder* staff **129** *miscarried* perished **131** *Hereford* i.e.
Bolingbroke

135   He ne'er had borne it out of Coventry.
For all the country in a general voice
Cried hate upon him, and all their prayers and love
Were set on Hereford, whom they doted on
And blessed and graced indeed, more than the king.]
But this is mere digression from my purpose.
Here come I from our princely general
To know your griefs, to tell you from his grace
That he will give you audience, and wherein
It shall appear that your demands are just,
145   You shall enjoy them, everything set off
That might so much as think you enemies.

MOWBRAY

But he hath forced us to compel this offer,
And it proceeds from policy, not love.

WESTMORELAND

149   Mowbray, you overween to take it so.
This offer comes from mercy, not from fear.
151   For, lo! within a ken our army lies,
Upon mine honor, all too confident
To give admittance to a thought of fear.
154   Our battle is more full of names than yours,
Our men more perfect in the use of arms,
Our armor all as strong, our cause the best.
157   Then reason will our hearts should be **as good.**
Say you not then our offer is compelled.

MOWBRAY

Well, by my will we shall admit no parley.

WESTMORELAND

That argues but the shame of your offense.
161   A rotten case abides no handling.

HASTINGS

Hath the Prince John a full commission,

---

35 *borne it* carried the prize; *Coventry* (where the combat took place)   145 *set off* removed   149 *overween* are presumptuous   151 *ken* range of vision   154 *battle . . . names* army has more leaders with distinguished reputations   157 *reason will* it is reasonable that   161 *rotten* weak

In very ample virtue of his father,   163
To hear and absolutely to determine
Of what conditions we shall stand upon?

WESTMORELAND
That is intended in the general's name.
I muse you make so slight a question.   167

ARCHBISHOP
Then take, my Lord of Westmoreland, this schedule,
For this contains our general grievances.
Each several article herein redressed,   170
All members of our cause, both here and hence,
That are insinewed to this action,   172
Acquitted by a true substantial form   173
And present execution of our wills
To us and to our purposes confined,
We come within our awful banks again   176
And knit our powers to the arm of peace.

WESTMORELAND
This will I show the general. Please you, lords,
In sight of both our battles we may meet,
And either end in peace – which God so frame –   180
Or to the place of difference call the swords   181
Which must decide it.

ARCHBISHOP   My lord, we will do so.
                                        Exit Westmoreland.

MOWBRAY
There is a thing within my bosom tells me
That no conditions of our peace can stand.

HASTINGS
Fear you not that. If we can make our peace
Upon such large terms and so absolute
As our conditions shall consist upon,
Our peace shall stand as firm as rocky mountains.

163 *In . . . virtue* by full authority 167 *muse* am surprised 170 *several* separate 172 *insinewed* joined by strong sinews 173 *substantial form* formal agreement 176 *banks* i.e. as a stream which has been in flood subsides to the confines of its banks 180 *frame* bring to pass 181 *difference* battle

MOWBRAY

189   Yea, but our valuation shall be such
      That every slight and false-derivèd cause,
191   Yea, every idle, nice, and wanton reason
      Shall to the king taste of this action,
193   That, were our royal faiths martyrs in love,
      We shall be winnowed with so rough a wind
      That even our corn shall seem as light as chaff
196   And good from bad find no partition.

ARCHBISHOP

      No, no, my lord. Note this. The king is weary
198   Of dainty and such picking grievances.
199   For he hath found to end one doubt by death
      Revives two greater in the heirs of life,
201   And therefore will he wipe his tables clean
      And keep no tell-tale to his memory
      That may repeat and history his loss
      To new remembrance. For full well he knows
205   He cannot so precisely weed this land
206   As his misdoubts present occasion.
      His foes are so enrooted with his friends
      That, plucking to unfix an enemy,
      He doth unfasten so and shake a friend.
      So that this land, like an offensive wife
      That hath enraged him on to offer strokes,
      As he is striking, holds his infant up
213   And hangs resolved correction in the arm
      That was upreared to execution.

HASTINGS

      Besides, the king hath wasted all his rods
      On late offenders, that he now doth lack

---

189 *our valuation* the king's valuation of us   191 *nice* petty; *wanton* frivolous 193 *That . . . love* so that even if we suffered martyrdom for our love of the king   196 *partition* distinction   198 *dainty* precise; *picking* trifling   199 *doubt* danger   201 *tables* note-book   205 *precisely* thoroughly   206 *misdoubts* suspicions   213–14 *hangs . . . execution* causes him to stay his arm and resolve upon correction rather than execution

The very instruments of chastisement.
So that his power, like to a fangless lion,
May offer, but not hold.   219

ARCHBISHOP   'Tis very true.
And therefore be assured, my good lord marshal,
If we do now make our atonement well,   221
Our peace will, like a broken limb united,
Grow stronger for the breaking.

MOWBRAY   Be it so.
Here is returned my Lord of Westmoreland.
     Enter Westmoreland.

WESTMORELAND
The prince is here at hand. Pleaseth your lordship
To meet his grace just distance 'tween our armies.   226

MOWBRAY
Your grace of York, in God's name then, set forward.

ARCHBISHOP
Before, and greet his grace, my lord; we come.   228

*

     Enter Prince John [of Lancaster] and his army.   IV, ii

LANCASTER
You are well encountered here, my cousin Mowbray.
Good day to you, gentle lord archbishop.
And so to you, Lord Hastings, and to all.
My Lord of York, it better showed with you
When that your flock, assembled by the bell,
Encircled you to hear with reverence
Your exposition on the holy text

219 *offer* threaten   **221** *atonement* reconciliation   **226** *just* exact   **228** *Before* go before
IV, ii (It is not certain that any change of scene was intended here. In the quarto the stage direction follows l. 226. The folio has instead 'Enter Prince John' following l. 228, which seems a better position. Neither stage direction indicates a change of scene; but the dialogue of ll. 227–28 seems to indicate that the stage was cleared after l. 228.)

8   Than now to see you here an iron man,
       Cheering a rout of rebels with your drum,
10   Turning the word to sword and life to death.
       That man that sits within a monarch's heart
       And ripens in the sunshine of his favor,
       Would he abuse the countenance of the king,
14   Alack, what mischiefs might he set abroach
       In shadow of such greatness. With you, lord bishop,
       It is even so. Who hath not heard it spoken
       How deep you were within the books of God?
       To us the speaker in His parliament,
       To us the imagined voice of God himself,
20   The very opener and intelligencer
       Between the grace, the sanctities of heaven
22   And our dull workings. O, who shall believe
       But you misuse the reverence of your place,
       Employ the countenance and grace of heaven,
       As a false favorite doth his prince's name,
26   In deeds dishonorable? You have ta'en up,
       Under the counterfeited zeal of God,
28   The subjects of His substitute, my father,
       And both against the peace of heaven and him
       Have here upswarmed them.
ARCHBISHOP   Good my Lord of Lancaster,
       I am not here against your father's peace,
       But, as I told my Lord of Westmoreland,
33   The time misordered doth, in common sense,
34   Crowd us and crush us to this monstrous form,
       To hold our safety up. I sent your grace
36   The parcels and particulars of our grief,
       The which hath been with scorn shoved from the court,
38   Whereon this Hydra son of war is born,

---

8 *an iron man* clad in armor   10 *the word* the Scripture   14 *abroach* afoot
20 *opener* interpreter; *intelligencer* messenger   22 *workings* operations of
the mind   26 *ta'en up* enlisted   28 *substitute* deputy   33 *common sense* the
judgment of all the people   34 *monstrous* unnatural   36 *parcels* details   38
Hydra many-headed

Whose dangerous eyes may well be charmed asleep
With grant of our most just and right desires,
And true obedience, of this madness cured,
Stoop tamely to the foot of majesty.

MOWBRAY
If not, we ready are to try our fortunes
To the last man.

HASTINGS   And though we here fall down,
We have supplies to second our attempt.   45
If they miscarry, theirs shall second them,
And so success of mischief shall be born   47
And heir from heir shall hold this quarrel up
Whiles England shall have generation.   49

LANCASTER
You are too shallow, Hastings, much too shallow,
To sound the bottom of the after-times.

WESTMORELAND
Pleaseth your grace to answer them directly
How far forth you do like their articles.

LANCASTER
I like them all, and do allow them well,
And swear here, by the honor of my blood,
My father's purposes have been mistook,
And some about him have too lavishly   57
Wrested his meaning and authority.   58
My lord, these griefs shall be with speed redressed,
Upon my soul, they shall. If this may please you,
Discharge your powers unto their several counties,
As we will ours. And here between the armies
Let's drink together friendly and embrace,
That all their eyes may bear those tokens home
Of our restorèd love and amity.

ARCHBISHOP
I take your princely word for these redresses.

45 *supplies* reinforcements; *second* take the place of   47 *success* succession
49 *generation* offspring   57 *lavishly* loosely   58 *Wrested* twisted

[LANCASTER]

I give it you, and will maintain my word.
And thereupon I drink unto your grace.

[HASTINGS]

Go, captain, and deliver to the army
70   This news of peace. Let them have pay, and part.
I know it will well please them. Hie thee, captain.

Exit [Officer].

ARCHBISHOP

To you, my noble Lord of Westmoreland.

WESTMORELAND

I pledge your grace, and, if you knew what pains
I have bestowed to breed this present peace,
You would drink freely. But my love to ye
Shall show itself more openly hereafter.

ARCHBISHOP

I do not doubt you.

WESTMORELAND   I am glad of it.

Health to my lord and gentle cousin, Mowbray.

MOWBRAY

You wish me health in very happy season,
80   For I am, on the sudden, something ill.

ARCHBISHOP

81   Against ill chances men are ever merry,
But heaviness foreruns the good event.

WESTMORELAND

Therefore be merry, coz, since sudden sorrow
Serves to say thus, 'Some good thing comes to-morrow.'

ARCHBISHOP

85   Believe me, I am passing light in spirit.

MOWBRAY

So much the worse, if your own rule be true.

Shouts [within].

---

70 *part* depart   **80** *something* somewhat   **81** *Against* in expectation of   **85**
passing exceedingly

LANCASTER
 The word of peace is rendered. Hark, how they shout!   87
MOWBRAY
 This had been cheerful after victory.
ARCHBISHOP
 A peace is of the nature of a conquest,
 For then both parties nobly are subdued,
 And neither party loser.
LANCASTER   Go, my lord,
 And let our army be dischargèd too.
                              [Exit Westmoreland.]
 And, good my lord, so please you, let our trains   93
 March by us, that we may peruse the men
 We should have coped withal.   95
ARCHBISHOP   Go, good Lord Hastings,
 And, ere they be dismissed, let them march by.
                              [Exit Hastings.]

LANCASTER
 I trust, lords, we shall lie to-night together.
        Enter Westmoreland.
 Now cousin, wherefore stands our army still?
WESTMORELAND
 The leaders, having charge from you to stand,
 Will not go off until they hear you speak.
LANCASTER
 They know their duties.
        Enter Hastings.
HASTINGS
 My lord, our army is dispersed already.
 Like youthful steers unyoked, they take their courses
 East, west, north, south, or, like a school broke up,
 Each hurries toward his home and sporting-place.   105
WESTMORELAND
 Good tidings, my Lord Hastings, for the which

87 *rendered* declared   93 *trains* armies   95 *coped withal* been matched with
105 *sporting-place* playground

I do arrest thee, traitor, of high treason.
And you, lord archbishop, and you, Lord Mowbray,
109   Of capital treason I attach you both.

MOWBRAY
Is this proceeding just and honorable?

WESTMORELAND
Is your assembly so?

ARCHBISHOP
Will you thus break your faith?

112 LANCASTER   I pawned thee none.
I promised you redress of these same grievances
Whereof you did complain, which, by mine honor,
I will perform with a most Christian care.
But for you, rebels, look to taste the due
Meet for rebellion and such acts as yours.
Most shallowly did you these arms commence,
119   Fondly brought here and foolishly sent hence.
120   Strike up our drums, pursue the scattered stray.
God, and not we, hath safely fought to-day.
Some guard these traitors to the block of death,
Treason's true bed and yielder up of breath.   *[Exeunt.]*

IV, iii   *Alarum. Excursions. Enter Falstaff [and Coleville,
                 meeting].*

1 FALSTAFF What's your name, sir? Of what condition are
you, and of what place, I pray?

COLEVILLE I am a knight, sir, and my name is Coleville
of the dale.

FALSTAFF Well, then, Coleville is your name, a knight is
your degree, and your place the dale. Coleville shall be
still your name, a traitor your degree, and the dungeon
your place, a place deep enough. So shall you be still
Coleville of the dale.

COLEVILLE Are not you Sir John Falstaff?

FALSTAFF As good a man as he, sir, whoe'er I am. Do ye

109 *capital* punishable by death   112 *pawned* pledged   119 *Fondly*
foolishly   120 *stray* stragglers
IV, iii   1 *condition* rank

yield, sir, or shall I sweat for you? If I do sweat, they are
the drops of thy lovers, and they weep for thy death. 13
Therefore rouse up fear and trembling, and do observ-
ance to my mercy.

COLEVILLE I think you are Sir John Falstaff, and in that
thought yield me.

FALSTAFF I have a whole school of tongues in this belly of 18
mine, and not a tongue of them all speaks any other word
but my name. An I had but a belly of any indifferency, I 20
were simply the most active fellow in Europe. My
womb, my womb, my womb undoes me. Here comes 22
our general.

> Enter [Prince] John [of Lancaster], Westmoreland,
> [Blunt,] and the rest. Retreat [sounded].

LANCASTER
The heat is past, follow no further now. 24
Call in the powers, good cousin Westmoreland.
> [Exit Westmoreland.]
Now, Falstaff, where have you been all this while?
When everything is ended, then you come.
These tardy tricks of yours will, on my life,
One time or other break some gallows' back.

FALSTAFF I would be sorry, my lord, but it should be
thus. I never knew yet but rebuke and check was the
reward of valor. Do you think me a swallow, an arrow, or
a bullet? Have I, in my poor and old motion, the expedition of thought? I have speeded hither with the very ex-
tremest inch of possibility. I have foundered nine score 35
and odd posts, and here, travel-tainted as I am, have, in 36
my pure and immaculate valor, taken Sir John Coleville
of the dale, a most furious knight and valorous enemy.
But what of that? He saw me, and yielded, that I may
justly say, with the hook-nosed fellow of Rome, their

---

13 *drops* tear-drops; *lovers* friends   18–20 *I . . . name* i.e. my corpulency
makes my identity unmistakable   18 *school* crowd   20 *indifferency*
moderate size   22 *womb* belly   24 *heat* height of the action   35 *foundered*
lamed   36 *posts* post-horses

Caesar, 'I came, saw, and overcame.'

LANCASTER It was more of his courtesy than your de-
serving.

FALSTAFF I know not. Here he is, and here I yield him.
And I beseech your grace, let it be booked with the rest
45   of this day's deeds, or, by the Lord, I will have it in a particular ballad else, with mine own picture on the top on't,
Coleville kissing my foot. To which course if I be
48   enforced, if you do not all show like gilt twopences to
me, and I in the clear sky of fame o'ershine you as much
50   as the full moon doth the cinders of the element, which
show like pins' heads to her, believe not the word of the
noble. Therefore let me have right, and let desert
mount.

LANCASTER Thine's too heavy to mount.

FALSTAFF Let it shine, then.

LANCASTER Thine's too thick to shine.

FALSTAFF Let it do something, my good lord, that may
do me good, and call it what you will.

LANCASTER Is thy name Coleville?

COLEVILLE It is, my lord.

LANCASTER A famous rebel art thou, Coleville.

FALSTAFF And a famous true subject took him.

COLEVILLE
I am, my lord, but as my betters are
That led me hither. Had they been ruled by me,
You should have won them dearer than you have.

FALSTAFF I know not how they sold themselves. But
thou, like a kind fellow, gavest thyself away gratis, and I
thank thee for thee.
        Enter Westmoreland.

LANCASTER
Now, have you left pursuit?

45–46 *particular ballad* broadside ballad celebrating my own exploits   48
show appear; *to* in comparison with   50 *cinders...element* stars

WESTMORELAND
    Retreat is made and execution stayed.   69

LANCASTER
    Send Coleville with his confederates
    To York, to present execution.   71
    Blunt, lead him hence, and see you guard him sure.
                    [*Exeunt Blunt and others with Coleville.*]
    And now dispatch we toward the court, my lords.   73
    I hear the king my father is sore sick.
    Our news shall go before us to his majesty,
    Which, cousin, you shall bear to comfort him,
    And we with sober speed will follow you.

FALSTAFF
    My lord, I beseech you give me leave to go
    Through Gloucestershire. And when you come to court,
    Stand my good lord, pray, in your good report.   80

LANCASTER
    Fare you well, Falstaff. I, in my condition,   81
    Shall better speak of you than you deserve.
                    [*Exeunt all but Falstaff.*]

FALSTAFF I would you had but the wit. 'Twere better than
your dukedom. Good faith, this same young sober-
blooded boy doth not love me, nor a man cannot make
him laugh. But that's no marvel, he drinks no wine.
There's never none of these demure boys come to any   87
proof, for thin drink doth so overcool their blood, and   88
making many fish-meals, that they fall into a kind of
male green-sickness, and then, when they marry, they get   90
wenches. They are generally fools and cowards, which
some of us should be too, but for inflammation. A good   92

---

69 *Retreat is made* the order for retreat has been given; *stayed* stopped **71**
present immediate **73** *dispatch we* let us hurry **80** *Stand . . . lord* be my
patron **81** *in my condition* i.e. as commanding officer **87–88** *come . . . proof*
stand up under testing **88** *thin drink* beer **90** *green-sickness* a form of
anemia, usually associated with young girls; *get* beget **92** *inflammation* i.e.
inflaming the mind with liquor

93   sherris-sack hath a twofold operation in it. It ascends me
into the brain, dries me there all the foolish and dull and
95 crudy vapors which environ it, makes it apprehensive,
96 quick, forgetive, full of nimble, fiery, and delectable
shapes, which, delivered o'er to the voice, the tongue,
98 which is the birth, becomes excellent wit. The second
property of your excellent sherris is the warming of the
100 blood, which, before cold and settled, left the liver white
and pale, which is the badge of pusillanimity and cowardice. But the sherris warms it and makes it course from
the inwards to the parts extremes. It illumineth the face,
which as a beacon gives warning to all the rest of this
105 little kingdom, man, to arm, and then the vital com-
moners and inland petty spirits muster me all to their
captain, the heart, who, great and puffed up with this
retinue, doth any deed of courage, and this valor comes
of sherris. So that skill in the weapon is nothing without
sack, for that sets it a-work, and learning a mere hoard of
111 gold kept by a devil, till sack commences it and sets it in
act and use. Hereof comes it that Prince Harry is valiant,
for the cold blood he did naturally inherit of his father,
114 he hath, like lean, sterile, and bare land, manured, hus-
banded, and tilled with excellent endeavor of drinking
good and good store of fertile sherris, that he is become
very hot and valiant. If I had a thousand sons, the first
humane principle I would teach them should be to forswear thin potations and to addict themselves to sack.
     Enter Bardolph.
   How now, Bardolph?
BARDOLPH   The army is discharged all and gone.

---

93 *sherris-sack* sherry   95 *crudy* curded; *apprehensive* discerning   96
forgetive inventive   98 *wit* understanding   100 *liver* (regarded as the seat of
courage)   105–06 *vital . . . spirits* vital spirits which inhabit man's inward
parts   111 *commences it* gives it license to act (as a university commence-
ment gives the graduate authority to put his knowledge to use)   114
manured cultivated

FALSTAFF Let them go. I'll through Gloucestershire, and
there will I visit Master Robert Shallow, esquire. I have 123
him already tempering between my finger and my
thumb, and shortly will I seal with him. Come away. 125
                                                [Exeunt.]

                              *

Enter the King, Warwick, Thomas Duke of Clarence, IV, iv
Humphrey [Duke] of Gloucester [, and others].

KING
    Now, lords, if God doth give successful end
    To this debate that bleedeth at our doors,   2
    We will our youth lead on to higher fields   3
    And draw no swords but what are sanctified.
    Our navy is addressed, our power collected,   5
    Our substitutes in absence well invested,   6
    And everything lies level to our wish.   7
    Only, we want a little personal strength,
    And pause us, till these rebels, now afoot,
    Come underneath the yoke of government.

WARWICK
    Both which we doubt not but your majesty
    Shall soon enjoy.

KING   Humphrey, my son of Gloucester,
    Where is the prince your brother?

GLOUCESTER
    I think he's gone to hunt, my lord, at Windsor.

KING
    And how accompanied?

GLOUCESTER   I do not know, my lord.

123–25 _I . . . thumb_ I am warming him, as sealing-wax is warmed between the
fingers 125 _seal with_ i.e. make use of
IV, iv Within King Henry's palace, Westminster 2 _debate_ quarrel 3–4
(for the king's intention to go on crusade to the Holy Land, see _1 Henry IV_,
I, i, 18–29) 5 _addressed_ ready 6 _substitutes_ deputies 7 _level to_ in accord-
ance with

KING

   Is not his brother, Thomas of Clarence, with him ?

GLOUCESTER

17   No, my good lord, he is in presence here.

CLARENCE

   What would my lord and father ?

KING

   Nothing but well to thee, Thomas of Clarence.

   How chance thou art not with the prince thy brother ?

   He loves thee, and thou dost neglect him, Thomas ;

   Thou hast a better place in his affection

   Than all thy brothers. Cherish it, my boy,

   And noble offices thou mayst effect

   Of mediation, after I am dead,

   Between his greatness and thy other brethren.

27   Therefore omit him not, blunt not his love,

   Nor lose the good advantage of his grace

   By seeming cold or careless of his will.

30   For he is gracious, if he be observed.

   He hath a tear for pity and a hand

32   Open as day for meting charity.

   Yet notwithstanding, being incensed, he's flint

34   As humorous as winter and as sudden

35   As flaws congealèd in the spring of day.

   His temper, therefore, must be well observed.

   Chide him for faults, and do it reverently,

   When you perceive his blood inclined to mirth,

   But, being moody, give him time and scope,

   Till that his passions, like a whale on ground,

41   Confound themselves with working. Learn this,

      Thomas,

   And thou shalt prove a shelter to thy friends,

   A hoop of gold to bind thy brothers in,

   That the united vessel of their blood,

---

17 *in presence* present at court   27 *omit* neglect   30 *observed* respected   32
meting distributing   34 *humorous* capricious   35 *flaws congealèd* snow-
flakes   41 *Confound* consume; *working* struggling

Mingled with venom of suggestion –   45
As, force perforce, the age will pour it in –
Shall never leak, though it do work as strong
As aconitum or rash gunpowder.   48

CLARENCE
I shall observe him with all care and love.

KING
Why art thou not at Windsor with him, Thomas?

CLARENCE
He is not there to-day; he dines in London.

KING
And how accompanied? Canst thou tell that?

CLARENCE
With Poins and other his continual followers.

KING
Most subject is the fattest soil to weeds,   54
And he, the noble image of my youth,
Is overspread with them. Therefore my grief
Stretches itself beyond the hour of death.
The blood weeps from my heart when I do shape
In forms imaginary the unguided days
And rotten times that you shall look upon
When I am sleeping with my ancestors.
For when his headstrong riot hath no curb,
When rage and hot blood are his counsellors,
When means and lavish manners meet together,   64
O, with what wings shall his affections fly
Towards fronting peril and opposed decay!   66

WARWICK
My gracious lord, you look beyond him quite.   67
The prince but studies his companions
Like a strange tongue, wherein, to gain the language,
'Tis needful that the most immodest word
Be looked upon and learned, which once attained,

45 *suggestion* false insinuation   48 *aconitum* monkshood, a violent poison;
rash quick and strong   54 *fattest* richest   64 *lavish* licentious   66 *fronting*
opposing; *decay* ruin   67 *look beyond* misunderstand

Your highness knows, comes to no further use
73 But to be known and hated. So, like gross terms,
74 The prince will in the perfectness of time
Cast off his followers, and their memory
Shall as a pattern or a measure live,
77 By which his grace must mete the lives of others,
Turning past evils to advantages.

KING
79 'Tis seldom when the bee doth leave her comb
In the dead carrion.

Enter Westmoreland.

                                    Who's here? Westmoreland?

WESTMORELAND
Health to my sovereign, and new happiness
Added to that that I am to deliver.
Prince John your son doth kiss your grace's hand.
Mowbray, the Bishop Scroop, Hastings and all
Are brought to the correction of your law.
There is not now a rebel's sword unsheathed,
But Peace puts forth her olive everywhere.
The manner how this action hath been borne
Here at more leisure may your highness read,
90 With every course in his particular.

KING
O Westmoreland, thou art a summer bird,
92 Which ever in the haunch of winter sings
The lifting up of day.

Enter Harcourt.

                                    Look, here's more news.

HARCOURT
From enemies heaven keep your majesty,
And, when they stand against you, may they fall
As those that I am come to tell you of!

73 *terms* expressions   74 *perfectness* perfection   77 *mete* appraise   79–80
'Tis ... carrion the bee which has placed her comb in a carcass seldom leaves
her honey   90 *every ... particular* every phase of the action set forth in
detail   92 *haunch* hinder part, end

The Earl Northumberland and the Lord Bardolph,
With a great power of English and of Scots,
Are by the shrieve of Yorkshire overthrown.   99
The manner and true order of the fight
This packet, please it you, contains at large.

KING
And wherefore should these good news make me sick?
Will Fortune never come with both hands full,
But write her fair words still in foulest letters?   104
She either gives a stomach and no food –
Such are the poor, in health – or else a feast
And takes away the stomach – such are the rich,
That have abundance and enjoy it not.
I should rejoice now at this happy news,
And now my sight fails, and my brain is giddy.
O me! Come near me. Now I am much ill.

GLOUCESTER
Comfort, your majesty!

CLARENCE   O my royal father!

WESTMORELAND
My sovereign lord, cheer up yourself, look up.

WARWICK
Be patient, princes. You do know these fits
Are with his highness very ordinary.
Stand from him, give him air, he'll straight be well.   116

CLARENCE
No, no, he cannot long hold out these pangs.   117
The incessant care and labor of his mind
Hath wrought the mure that should confine it in   119
So thin that life looks through and will break out.

GLOUCESTER
The people fear me, for they do observe   121
Unfathered heirs and loathly births of nature.   122

---

99 *shrieve* sheriff **104** *still* ever **116** *straight* straightway **117** *hold out*
endure **119** *wrought the mure* made the wall **121** *fear* frighten **122** *Unfathered heirs* persons thought to be supernaturally conceived; *loathly births*
monstrous infants

The seasons change their manners, as the year
Had found some months asleep and leaped them over.

CLARENCE
125   The river hath thrice flowed, no ebb between,
And the old folk, time's doting chronicles,
Say it did so a little time before
128   That our great-grandsire, Edward, sicked and died.

WARWICK
Speak lower, princes, for the king recovers.

GLOUCESTER
This apoplexy will certain be his end.

KING
I pray you, take me up, and bear me hence
132   Into some other chamber. Softly, pray.
      [They bear him to another place.]

IV, v   Let there be no noise made, my gentle friends,
2   Unless some dull and favorable hand
Will whisper music to my weary spirit.

WARWICK
Call for the music in the other room.

KING
Set me the crown upon my pillow here.

CLARENCE
6   His eye is hollow, and he changes much.

WARWICK
Less noise, less noise!
          Enter Prince Henry.

PRINCE   Who saw the Duke of Clarence?

CLARENCE
I am here, brother, full of heaviness.

PRINCE
9   How now! Rain within doors, and none abroad!

125 *river* Thames   128 *Edward* Edward III   132 *Into some other chamber*
(the king remains in view, and so was perhaps borne to a bed placed at some
other point on the stage)
IV, v   2 *dull* soothing; *favorable* kindly   **6** *changes* grows pale   **9** *Rain*
i.e. tears

How doth the king?

GLOUCESTER
Exceeding ill.

PRINCE   Heard he the good news yet?
Tell it him.

GLOUCESTER
He altered much upon the hearing it.

PRINCE
If he be sick with joy, he'll recover without physic.

WARWICK
Not so much noise, my lords. Sweet prince, speak low.
The king your father is disposed to sleep.

CLARENCE
Let us withdraw into the other room.

WARWICK
Will't please your grace to go along with us?

PRINCE
No, I will sit and watch here by the king.
               [Exeunt all but the Prince.]
Why doth the crown lie there upon his pillow,
Being so troublesome a bedfellow?
O polished perturbation! Golden care!   22
That keep'st the ports of slumber open wide   23
To many a watchful night! Sleep with it now!
Yet not so sound and half so deeply sweet
As he whose brow with homely biggen bound   26
Snores out the watch of night. O majesty!
When thou dost pinch thy bearer, thou dost sit
Like a rich armor worn in heat of day,
That scald'st with safety. By his gates of breath   30
There lies a downy feather which stirs not.
Did he suspire, that light and weightless down   32
Perforce must move. My gracious lord! my father!
This sleep is sound indeed. This is a sleep

22 *perturbation* cause of perturbation   23 *ports* gates   26 *biggen* nightcap
30 *scald'st with safety* burns while it protects; *gates of breath* lips   32
suspire breathe

35 That from this golden rigol hath divorced
So many English kings. Thy due from me
Is tears and heavy sorrows of the blood,
Which nature, love, and filial tenderness
Shall, O dear father, pay thee plenteously.
My due from thee is this imperial crown,
41 Which, as immediate from thy place and blood,
42 Derives itself to me. *[Puts on the crown.]* Lo, where it sits,
Which God shall guard. And put the world's whole strength
Into one giant arm, it shall not force
45 This lineal honor from me. This from thee
Will I to mine leave, as 'tis left to me. *[Exit.]*

KING
Warwick! Gloucester! Clarence!
Enter Warwick, Gloucester, Clarence.

CLARENCE
Doth the king call?

WARWICK
What would your majesty? How fares your grace?

KING
Why did you leave me here alone, my lords?

CLARENCE
We left the prince my brother here, my liege,
Who undertook to sit and watch by you.

KING
The Prince of Wales! Where is he? Let me see him.
He is not here.

WARWICK
The door is open; he is gone this way.

GLOUCESTER
He came not through the chamber where we stayed.

KING
Where is the crown? Who took it from my pillow?

35 *rigol* circle   41 *immediate from* nearest to   42 *Derives* descends   45 *lineal* inherited

WARWICK
When we withdrew, my liege, we left it here.

KING
The prince hath ta'en it hence. Go, seek him out.
Is he so hasty that he doth suppose
My sleep my death?
Find him, my Lord of Warwick, chide him hither.
                                        [Exit Warwick.]
This part of his conjoins with my disease   63
And helps to end me. See, sons, what things you are!
How quickly nature falls into revolt
When gold becomes her object!
For this the foolish overcareful fathers
Have broke their sleep with thoughts, their brains with   68
    care,
Their bones with industry.
For this they have engrossed and pilèd up   70
The cankered heaps of strange-achievèd gold;   71
For this they have been thoughtful to invest   72
Their sons with arts and martial exercises.   73
When, like the bee, tolling from every flower   74
[The virtuous sweets],
Our thighs packed with wax, our mouths with honey,
We bring it to the hive, and, like the bees,
Are murdered for our pains. This bitter taste   78
Yields his engrossments to the ending father.   79
        Enter Warwick.
Now, where is he that will not stay so long
Till his friend sickness hath determined me?   81

WARWICK
My lord, I found the prince in the next room,
Washing with kindly tears his gentle cheeks,   83

---

63 *part* conduct **68** *thoughts* anxieties **70** *engrossed* accumulated **71**
cankered tarnished **72** *thoughtful* careful **73** *arts* learning **74** *tolling*
gathering **78–79** *This . . . engrossments* his accumulations leave this bitter
taste **79** *ending* dying **81** *determined* put an end to **83** *kindly* natural

84 With such a deep demeanor in great sorrow
That tyranny, which never quaffed but blood,
Would, by beholding him, have washed his knife
With gentle eye-drops. He is coming hither.

KING
But wherefore did he take away the crown?
      Enter [Prince] Henry.
Lo, where he comes. Come hither to me, Harry.
Depart the chamber, leave us here alone.
              Exeunt [Warwick and the rest].

PRINCE
I never thought to hear you speak again.

KING
Thy wish was father, Harry, to that thought.
I stay too long by thee, I weary thee.
Dost thou so hunger for mine empty chair
That thou wilt needs invest thee with my honors
Before thy hour be ripe? O foolish youth!
Thou seek'st the greatness that will overwhelm thee.
Stay but a little, for my cloud of dignity
Is held from falling with so weak a wind
That it will quickly drop. My day is dim.
Thou hast stolen that which after some few hours
Were thine without offense, and at my death
103 Thou hast sealed up my expectation.
Thy life did manifest thou lovedst me not,
And thou wilt have me die assured of it.
Thou hidest a thousand daggers in thy thoughts,
Which thou hast whetted on thy stony heart,
To stab at half an hour of my life.
What! Canst thou not forbear me half an hour?
Then get thee gone and dig my grave thyself,
And bid the merry bells ring to thine ear
That thou art crownèd, not that I am dead.
Let all the tears that should bedew my hearse

84 *deep* intense   103 *sealed up* confirmed

Be drops of balm to sanctify thy head.   114
Only compound me with forgotten dust;   115
Give that which gave thee life unto the worms.
Pluck down my officers, break my decrees,
For now a time is come to mock at form.   118
Harry the Fifth is crowned. Up, vanity!   119
Down, royal state! All you sage counsellors, hence!
And to the English court assemble now,
From every region, apes of idleness!
Now, neighbor confines, purge you of your scum.   123
Have you a ruffian that will swear, drink, dance,
Revel the night, rob, murder, and commit
The oldest sins the newest kind of ways?
Be happy, he will trouble you no more.
England shall double gild his treble guilt,
England shall give him office, honor, might,
For the fifth Harry from curbed license plucks
The muzzle of restraint, and the wild dog
Shall flesh his tooth on every innocent.   132
O my poor kingdom, sick with civil blows!
When that my care could not withhold thy riots,   134
What wilt thou do when riot is thy care?   135
O, thou wilt be a wilderness again,
Peopled with wolves, thy old inhabitants.

PRINCE

O, pardon me, my liege! But for my tears,
The moist impediments unto my speech,
I had forestalled this dear and deep rebuke   140
Ere you with grief had spoke and I had heard
The course of it so far. There is your crown,
And He that wears the crown immortally
Long guard it yours. If I affect it more   144
Than as your honor and as your renown,

---

114 *balm* oil of consecration   115 *compound* mix   118 *form* ceremony   119
vanity folly   123 *confines* regions   132 *flesh* plunge into flesh   134 *care*
carefulness   135 *care* occupation   140 *dear* severe   144 *affect* desire

146   Let me no more from this obedience rise,
Which my most inward true and duteous spirit
Teacheth, this prostrate and exterior bending.
God witness with me, when I here came in,
And found no course of breath within your majesty,
How cold it struck my heart. If I do feign,
O, let me in my present wildness die
And never live to show the incredulous world
The noble change that I have purposèd.
Coming to look on you, thinking you dead,
And dead almost, my liege, to think you were,
I spake unto this crown as having sense,
And thus upbraided it : 'The care on thee depending
Hath fed upon the body of my father.
Therefore, thou best of gold art worst of gold.
Other, less fine in carat, is more precious,
162   Preserving life in medicine potable,
But thou, most fine, most honored, most renowned,
Hast eat thy bearer up.' Thus, my most royal liege,
Accusing it, I put it on my head,
To try with it, as with an enemy
That had before my face murdered my father,
The quarrel of a true inheritor.
But if it did infect my blood with joy,
170   Or swell my thoughts to any strain of pride,
If any rebel or vain spirit of mine
Did with the least affection of a welcome
Give entertainment to the might of it,
Let God for ever keep it from my head
And make me as the poorest vassal is
That doth with awe and terror kneel to it.

KING

[O my son,]
God put it in thy mind to take it hence,

146 *obedience* obeisance, low curtsy   162 *medicine potable* (gold in solution was often prescribed as a medicine)   170 *strain* feeling

That thou mightst win the more thy father's love,
Pleading so wisely in excuse of it!
Come hither, Harry, sit thou by my bed,
And hear, I think, the very latest counsel   182
That ever I shall breathe. God knows, my son,
By what bypaths and indirect crooked ways
I met this crown, and I myself know well
How troublesome it sat upon my head.
To thee it shall descend with better quiet,
Better opinion, better confirmation,   188
For all the soil of the achievement goes   189
With me into the earth. It seemed in me
But as an honor snatched with boisterous hand,
And I had many living to upbraid
My gain of it by their assistances,
Which daily grew to quarrel and to bloodshed
Wounding supposèd peace. All these bold fears   195
Thou seest with peril I have answerèd,
For all my reign hath been but as a scene
Acting that argument. And now my death   198
Changes the mode, for what in me was purchased   199
Falls upon thee in a more fairer sort,
So thou the garland wear'st successively.   201
Yet, though thou stand'st more sure than I could do,
Thou art not firm enough, since griefs are green.   203
And all my friends, which thou must make thy friends,
Have but their stings and teeth newly ta'en out,
By whose fell working I was first advanced   206
And by whose power I well might lodge a fear   207
To be again displaced. Which to avoid,
I cut them off, and had a purpose now
To lead out many to the Holy Land,

182 *latest* last   188 *opinion* reputation   189 *soil* stain   195 *bold fears* grave
dangers   198 *argument* theme   199 *mode* musical key, mood; *purchased*
acquired by my own act   201 *garland* crown; *successively* by hereditary
right   203 *griefs are green* grievances are fresh   206 *fell* fierce   207 *lodge*
harbor

211   Lest rest and lying still might make them look
        Too near unto my state. Therefore, my Harry,
        Be it thy course to busy giddy minds
214   With foreign quarrels, that action, hence borne out,
        May waste the memory of the former days.
        More would I, but my lungs are wasted so
        That strength of speech is utterly denied me.
        How I came by the crown, O God forgive,
        And grant it may with thee in true peace live!

PRINCE
        [My gracious liege,]
        You won it, wore it, kept it, gave it me.
        Then plain and right must my possession be,
223   Which I with more than with a common pain
        'Gainst all the world will rightfully maintain.

           Enter [Prince John of] Lancaster [and Warwick].

KING
        Look, look, here comes my John of Lancaster.

LANCASTER
        Health, peace, and happiness to my royal father!

KING
        Thou bring'st me happiness and peace, son John,
        But health, alack, with youthful wings is flown
        From this bare withered trunk. Upon thy sight
        My worldly business makes a period.
        Where is my Lord of Warwick?

PRINCE   My Lord of Warwick!

KING
        Doth any name particular belong
        Unto the lodging where I first did swoon?

WARWICK
234   'Tis called Jerusalem, my noble lord.

KING
        Laud be to God! Even there my life must end.

211–12 *look ... near* examine too closely   **214** *action ... out* military action waged abroad   **223** *pain* effort   **234** *Jerusalem* (actually in Westminster Abbey rather than in the palace)

It hath been prophesied to me many years
I should not die but in Jerusalem,
Which vainly I supposed the Holy Land.
But bear me to that chamber; there I'll lie.
In that Jerusalem shall Harry die.   *[Exeunt.]*

*

Enter Shallow, Falstaff, and Bardolph [and Page].   V, i

SHALLOW By cock and pie, sir, you shall not away to-   1
night. What, Davy, I say!

FALSTAFF You must excuse me, Master Robert Shallow.

SHALLOW I will not excuse you, you shall not be excused,
excuses shall not be admitted, there is no excuse shall
serve, you shall not be excused. Why, Davy!

Enter Davy.

DAVY Here, sir.

SHALLOW Davy, Davy, Davy, Davy, let me see, Davy.
Let me see, Davy, let me see. Yea, marry, William cook,
bid him come hither. Sir John, you shall not be excused.

DAVY Marry, sir, thus, those precepts cannot be served.   11
And, again, sir, shall we sow the headland with wheat?   12

SHALLOW With red wheat, Davy. But for William cook –
are there no young pigeons?

DAVY Yes, sir. Here is now the smith's note for shoeing   15
and plough-irons.

SHALLOW Let it be cast and paid. Sir John, you shall not   17
be excused.

DAVY Now, sir, a new link to the bucket must needs be   19
had. And, sir, do you mean to stop any of William's
wages, about the sack he lost the other day at Hinckley
fair?

SHALLOW 'A shall answer it. Some pigeons, Davy, a   23
couple of short-legged hens, a joint of mutton, and any

V, i Shallow's house in Gloucestershire   1 *By cock and pie* (a mild oath)
11 *precepts* orders   12 *headland* unploughed strip between two ploughed
fields   15 *note* bill   17 *cast* verified   19 *bucket* yoke   23 *answer* pay for

25   pretty little tiny kickshaws, tell William cook.

DAVY Doth the man of war stay all night, sir?

SHALLOW Yea, Davy. I will use him well. A friend i' th'
court is better than a penny in purse. Use his men well,
Davy, for they are arrant knaves and will backbite.

30 DAVY No worse than they are backbitten, sir, for they
have marvellous foul linen.

32 SHALLOW Well conceited, Davy. About thy business,
Davy.

34 DAVY I beseech you, sir, to countenance William Visor of
35   Woncot against Clement Perkes o' th' hill.

SHALLOW There is many complaints, Davy, against that
Visor. That Visor is an arrant knave, on my knowledge.

DAVY I grant your worship that he is a knave, sir, but yet,
God forbid, sir, but a knave should have some countenance at his friend's request. An honest man, sir, is able
to speak for himself, when a knave is not. I have served
your worship truly, sir, this eight years, and if I cannot
42   once or twice in a quarter bear out a knave against an
honest man, I have but a very little credit with your worship. The knave is mine honest friend, sir. Therefore, I
beseech you, let him be countenanced.

46 SHALLOW Go to, I say he shall have no wrong. Look
about, Davy. *[Exit Davy.]* Where are you, Sir John?
Come, come, come, off with your boots. Give me your
hand, Master Bardolph.

BARDOLPH I am glad to see your worship.

SHALLOW I thank thee with all my heart, kind Master
Bardolph. *[to the Page]* And welcome, my tall fellow.
Come, Sir John.

FALSTAFF I'll follow you, good Master Robert Shallow.
[Exit Shallow.] Bardolph, look to our horses. *[Exeunt*
56   *Bardolph and Page.]* If I were sawed into quantities, I

25 *kickshaws* delicacies   30 *backbitten* i.e. by vermin   32 *Well conceited*
wittily said   34 *countenance* favor   34, 35 *Visor, Perkes* familiar Gloucestershire names in Shakespeare's day   42 *quarter* i.e. of a year; *bear out* support
46–47 *Look about* on your toes!   56 *quantities* small pieces

should make four dozen of such bearded hermits' staves
as Master Shallow. It is a wonderful thing to see the sem- 58
blable coherence of his men's spirits and his. They, by
observing him, do bear themselves like foolish justices;
he, by conversing with them, is turned into a justice-like
serving-man. Their spirits are so married in conjunction
with the participation of society that they flock together 63
in consent, like so many wild geese. If I had a suit to 64
Master Shallow, I would humor his men with the impu-
tation of being near their master. If to his men, I would
curry with Master Shallow that no man could better
command his servants. It is certain that either wise bearing or ignorant carriage is caught, as men take diseases,
one of another. Therefore let men take heed of their company. I will devise matter enough out of this Shallow to
keep Prince Harry in continual laughter the wearing out
of six fashions, which is four terms, or two actions, and 73
'a shall laugh without intervallums. O, it is much that a lie 74
with a slight oath and a jest with a sad brow will do with 75
a fellow that never had the ache in his shoulders! O, you
shall see him laugh till his face be like a wet cloak ill laid 77
up!

SHALLOW *[within]* Sir John!

FALSTAFF I come, Master Shallow, I come, Master
Shallow.   *[Exit.]*

*

Enter Warwick, [meeting the] Lord Chief Justice.   V, ii

WARWICK
How now, my lord chief justice! whither away?

58–59 *semblable coherence* similarity   63 *the participation of society* **close**
association   64 *consent* unanimity   73 *four terms* i.e. a year, since there are
four 'terms' in the legal year; *actions* suits for the recovery of debt   74
intervallums interruptions (literally, intervals between legal 'terms')   75
sad serious   77–78 *ill laid up* i.e. full of wrinkles
V, ii Within King Henry's palace

CHIEF JUSTICE
How doth the king?
WARWICK
Exceeding well. His cares are now all ended.
CHIEF JUSTICE
I hope, not dead.
WARWICK   He's walked the way of nature,
And to our purposes he lives no more.
CHIEF JUSTICE
I would his majesty had called me with him.
7   The service that I truly did his life
Hath left me open to all injuries.
WARWICK
Indeed I think the young king loves you not.
CHIEF JUSTICE
I know he doth not, and do arm myself
To welcome the condition of the time,
Which cannot look more hideously upon me
13   Than I have drawn it in my fantasy.
            Enter [Prince] John [of Lancaster], Thomas
            [of Clarence], and Humphrey [of Gloucester,
            with Westmoreland].
WARWICK
14   Here come the heavy issue of dead Harry.
O that the living Harry had the temper
Of him, the worst of these three gentlemen!
How many nobles then should hold their places
18   That must strike sail to spirits of vile sort!
CHIEF JUSTICE
O God, I fear all will be overturned!
LANCASTER
Good morrow, cousin Warwick, good morrow.
GLOUCESTER, CLARENCE
Good morrow, cousin.

---

7 *truly* faithfully   13 *fantasy* fancy   14 *heavy issue* sorrowing sons   18
strike sail i.e. submit themselves

LANCASTER
  We meet like men that had forgot to speak.

WARWICK
  We do remember, but our argument
  Is all too heavy to admit much talk.

LANCASTER
  Well, peace be with him that hath made us heavy.

CHIEF JUSTICE
  Peace be with us, lest we be heavier.

GLOUCESTER
  O, good my lord, you have lost a friend indeed,
  And I dare swear you borrow not that face
  Of seeming sorrow, it is sure your own.

LANCASTER
  Though no man be assured what grace to find,   30
  You stand in coldest expectation.   31
  I am the sorrier. Would 'twere otherwise.

CLARENCE
  Well, you must now speak Sir John Falstaff fair,
  Which swims against your stream of quality.   34

CHIEF JUSTICE
  Sweet princes, what I did, I did in honor,
  Led by the impartial conduct of my soul,
  And never shall you see that I will beg   37
  A ragged and forestalled remission.
  If truth and upright innocency fail me,
  I'll to the king my master that is dead,
  And tell him who hath sent me after him.

WARWICK
  Here comes the prince.
     Enter the Prince [as King Henry the Fifth] and Blunt.

CHIEF JUSTICE
  Good morrow, and God save your majesty!

---

23 *argument* situation   30 *grace to find* favor he will find   31 *coldest* gloomiest   34 *swims . . . stream of* goes against the grain of your   37–38 *beg . . . remission* ask pardon, like a ragged beggar, for an offense I have not committed

KING

This new and gorgeous garment, majesty,
Sits not so easy on me as you think.
Brothers, you mix your sadness with some fear.
This is the English, not the Turkish court.
48   Not Amurath an Amurath succeeds,
But Harry Harry. Yet be sad, good brothers,
For, by my faith, it very well becomes you.
Sorrow so royally in you appears
52   That I will deeply put the fashion on
And wear it in my heart. Why then, be sad,
But entertain no more of it, good brothers,
Than a joint burden laid upon us all.
For me, by heaven, I bid you be assured,
I'll be your father and your brother too.
Let me but bear your love, I'll bear your cares.
Yet weep that Harry's dead, and so will I,
But Harry lives, that shall convert those tears
By number into hours of happiness.

PRINCES

We hope no other from your majesty.

KING

63   You all look strangely on me.
      [To the Chief Justice]   And you most.
You are, I think, assured I love you not.

CHIEF JUSTICE

65   I am assured, if I be measured rightly,
Your majesty hath no just cause to hate me.

KING

No?
How might a prince of my great hopes forget
So great indignities you laid upon me?

---

48 *Amurath* a Turkish sultan who, upon his accession, caused all his brothers to be strangled   **52** *deeply* solemnly   **63** *strangely* suspiciously
65 *measured* judged

What! Rate, rebuke, and roughly send to prison   70
The immediate heir of England! Was this easy?   71
May this be washed in Lethe, and forgotten?

CHIEF JUSTICE

I then did use the person of your father.   73
The image of his power lay then in me.   74
And, in the administration of his law,
Whiles I was busy for the commonwealth,
Your highness pleasèd to forget my place,
The majesty and power of law and justice,
The image of the king whom I presented,   79
And struck me in my very seat of judgement.
Whereon, as an offender to your father,
I gave bold way to my authority
And did commit you. If the deed were ill,   83
Be you contented, wearing now the garland,
To have a son set your decrees at nought,
To pluck down justice from your awful bench,   86
To trip the course of law and blunt the sword
That guards the peace and safety of your person,
Nay, more, to spurn at your most royal image
And mock your workings in a second body.   90
Question your royal thoughts, make the case yours.
Be now the father and propose a son,   92
Hear your own dignity so much profaned,
See your most dreadful laws so loosely slighted,
Behold yourself so by a son disdained,
And then imagine me taking your part
And in your power soft silencing your son.

---

70 *Rate* chide; *send to prison* (the story of Prince Hal's imprisonment for striking the Chief Justice was first told in Sir Thomas Elyot's *The Book Named the Governor*, 1531) **71** *easy* insignificant **73** *use the person* perform the function **74** *image* symbol **79** *presented* represented **83** *commit* commit to prison **86** *awful* awesome **90** *your . . . body* the actions of your deputy **92** *propose* imagine

98   After this cold considerance, sentence me,

99   And, as you are a king, speak in your state
What I have done that misbecame my place,
My person, or my liege's sovereignty.

KING

You are right, justice, and you weigh this well.
Therefore still bear the balance and the sword.
And I do wish your honors may increase,
Till you do live to see a son of mine
Offend you and obey you, as I did.
So shall I live to speak my father's words:
'Happy am I, that have a man so bold
That dares do justice on my proper son,
And not less happy, having such a son
That would deliver up his greatness so
Into the hands of justice.' You did commit me.
For which, I do commit into your hand
The unstained sword that you have used to bear,

115   With this remembrance, that you use the same
With the like bold, just, and impartial spirit
As you have done 'gainst me. There is my hand.
You shall be as a father to my youth.

119   My voice shall sound as you do prompt mine ear,
And I will stoop and humble my intents
To your well-practiced wise directions.
And, princes all, believe me, I beseech you,

123   My father is gone wild into his grave,

124   For in his tomb lie my affections,
And with his spirit sadly I survive,
To mock the expectation of the world,
To frustrate prophecies and to raze out
Rotten opinion, who hath writ me down

129   After my seeming. The tide of blood in me

---

98 *cold considerance* cool consideration   **99** *state* royal capacity   **115** *remembrance* reminder   **119** *sound* speak   **123** *My . . . grave* i.e. my wildness is buried with my father   **124** *affections* wayward propensities   **129** *seeming* outward appearance

Hath proudly flowed in vanity till now.
Now doth it turn and ebb back to the sea,
Where it shall mingle with the state of floods   132
And flow henceforth in formal majesty.
Now call we our high court of parliament.
And let us choose such limbs of noble counsel
That the great body of our state may go
In equal rank with the best-governed nation ;
That war, or peace, or both at once, may be
As things acquainted and familiar to us,
In which you, father, shall have foremost hand.
Our coronation done, we will accite,   141
As I before remembered, all our state.   142
And, God consigning to my good intents,   143
No prince nor peer shall have just cause to say,
God shorten Harry's happy life one day !   *Exeunt.*

*

*Enter Sir John [Falstaff], Shallow, Silence, Davy,   V, ii
Bardolph, Page.*

SHALLOW Nay, you shall see my orchard, where, in an
arbor, we will eat a last year's pippin of my own graffing,   2
with a dish of caraways, and so forth. Come, cousin   3
Silence. And then to bed.

FALSTAFF 'Fore God, you have here a goodly dwelling
and a rich.

SHALLOW Barren, barren, barren. Beggars all, beggars
all, Sir John. Marry, good air. Spread, Davy, spread,   8
Davy. Well said, Davy.   9

FALSTAFF This Davy serves you for good uses. He is
your serving-man and your husband.   11

132 *state of floods* majesty of the sea   141 *accite* summon   142 *remembered*
mentioned; *state* nobles and great men of the realm   143 *consigning* agreeing
V, iii Within Shallow's orchard   2 *pippin* a variety of apple; *graffing*
grafting   3 *caraways* caraway seeds   8 *Spread* lay the table   9 *said* done
11 *husband* steward

12 SHALLOW A good varlet, a good varlet, a very good varlet, Sir John. By the mass, I have drunk too much sack
at supper. A good varlet. Now sit down, now sit down.
Come, cousin.

16 SILENCE Ah, sirrah! quoth-a, we shall
          [Sings]
                    Do nothing but eat, and make good cheer,
                    And praise God for the merry year,
19   When flesh is cheap and females dear,
                    And lusty lads roam here and there
                              So merrily,
                    And ever among so merrily.

FALSTAFF There's a merry heart! Good Master Silence,
I'll give you a health for that anon.

SHALLOW Give Master Bardolph some wine, Davy.

DAVY Sweet sir, sit, I'll be with you anon. Most sweet sir,
27   sit. Master page, good master page, sit. Proface! What
28   you want in meat, we'll have in drink. But you must
29   bear, the heart's all.   *[Exit.]*

SHALLOW Be merry, Master Bardolph, and, my little
soldier there, be merry.

SILENCE *[sings]*
                    Be merry, be merry, my wife has all,
                    For women are shrews, both short and tall.
                    'Tis merry in hall when beards wag all,
35   And welcome merry Shrove-tide.
                    Be merry, be merry.

FALSTAFF I did not think Master Silence had been a man
of this mettle.

SILENCE Who, I? I have been merry twice and once ere
now.

          Enter Davy.

40 DAVY *[to Bardolph]* There's a dish of leather-coats for you.

SHALLOW Davy!

---

12 *varlet* servant   **16** *quoth-a* said he   **19** *flesh* meat   **27** *Proface* a form of
welcome at dinner   **28** *want* lack   **29** *bear* be patient   **35** *Shrove-tide*
season of feasting before Lent   **40** *leather-coats* russet apples

DAVY Your worship! *[to Bardolph]* I'll be with you
   straight. – A cup of wine, sir?

SILENCE *[sings]*

> A cup of wine that's brisk and fine,
> And drink unto the leman mine,   45
>   And a merry heart lives long-a.

FALSTAFF Well said, Master Silence.

SILENCE An we shall be merry, now comes in the sweet o'
   the night.

FALSTAFF Health and long life to you, Master Silence.

SILENCE *[sings]*

> Fill the cup, and let it come,
> I'll pledge you a mile to the bottom.

SHALLOW Honest Bardolph, welcome. If thou want'st
   anything, and wilt not call, beshrew thy heart. *[to the* 54
   Page] Welcome, my little tiny thief, and welcome indeed too. I'll drink to Master Bardolph, and to all the
   cabileros about London.   57

DAVY I hope to see London once ere I die.

BARDOLPH An I might see you there, Davy –

SHALLOW By the mass, you'll crack a quart together, ha!
   Will you not, Master Bardolph?

BARDOLPH Yea, sir, in a pottle-pot.   62

SHALLOW By God's liggens, I thank thee. The knave will 63
   stick by thee, I can assure thee that. 'A will not out, he is 64
   true bred.

BARDOLPH And I'll stick by him, sir.

> *One knocks at door.*

SHALLOW Why, there spoke a king. Lack nothing. Be
   merry. Look who's at door there, ho! Who knocks?

>   *[Exit Davy.]*

FALSTAFF *[to Silence, seeing him drinking]* Why, now you
   have done me right.   70

---

45 *leman* sweetheart   **54** *beshrew* the devil take   **57** *cabileros* gallants   **62**
pottle-pot two quart tankard   **63** *By God's liggens* (this oath has not been
satisfactorily explained)   **64** *'A … out* he won't pass out   **70** *done me right*
drunk even with me

SILENCE *[sings]*
>   Do me right,
>   And dub me knight.
>   Samingo.
73

Is't not so?

FALSTAFF 'Tis so.

SILENCE Is't so? Why then, say an old man can do somewhat.

[Enter Davy.]

DAVY An't please your worship, there's one Pistol come
from the court with news.

FALSTAFF From the court! Let him come in.

Enter Pistol.

How now, Pistol!

PISTOL Sir John, God save you!

FALSTAFF What wind blew you hither, Pistol?

PISTOL Not the ill wind which blows no man to good.
Sweet knight, thou art now one of the greatest men in
this realm.

87 SILENCE By'r lady, I think 'a be, but goodman Puff of
Barson.

PISTOL Puff!

Puff i' thy teeth, most recreant coward base!
Sir John, I am thy Pistol and thy friend,
And helter-skelter have I rode to thee,
And tidings do I bring and lucky joys
And golden times and happy news of price.

FALSTAFF I pray thee now, deliver them like a man of this
world.

PISTOL

97   A foutra for the world and worldlings base!
I speak of Africa and golden joys.

FALSTAFF

99   O base Assyrian knight, what is thy news?

---

73 *Samingo* Sir Mingo, the hero of the song   **87** *but* except; *goodman*
yeoman   **97** *foutra* an indecent term of contempt   **99** *Assyrian* i.e. heathen

Let King Cophetua know the truth thereof.   100

SILENCE [sings]
And Robin Hood, Scarlet, and John.

PISTOL
Shall dunghill curs confront the Helicons?   102
And shall good news be baffled?   103
Then, Pistol, lay thy head in Furies' lap.

SHALLOW Honest gentleman, I know not your breeding.

PISTOL Why then, lament therefore.   106

SHALLOW Give me pardon, sir. If, sir, you come with
news from the court, I take it there's but two ways,
either to utter them, or to conceal them. I am, sir, under
the king, in some authority.

PISTOL
Under which king, Besonian? Speak, or die.   111

SHALLOW
Under King Harry.

PISTOL   Harry the Fourth? or Fifth?

SHALLOW
Harry the Fourth.

PISTOL   A foutra for thine office!
Sir John, thy tender lambkin now is king.
Harry the Fifth's the man. I speak the truth.
When Pistol lies, do this, and fig me, like   116
The bragging Spaniard.

FALSTAFF
What, is the old king dead?

PISTOL
As nail in door. The things I speak are just.

FALSTAFF Away, Bardolph! Saddle my horse. Master
Robert Shallow, choose what office thou wilt in the
land, 'tis thine. Pistol, I will double-charge thee with 122

---

100 *Cophetua* (an allusion to the ballad of the king who married a beggar-
maid) 102 *Helicons* poets 103 *baffled* disgraced 106 *therefore* on that
account 111 *Besonian* knave 116 *fig* insult by putting the thumb
between the index and third fingers 122 *double-charge* (another play on
Pistol's name)

dignities.

BARDOLPH
O joyful day!
I would not take a knighthood for my fortune.

PISTOL
What! I do bring good news.

FALSTAFF Carry Master Silence to bed. Master Shallow,
my Lord Shallow – be what thou wilt, I am fortune's
steward – get on thy boots. We'll ride all night. O sweet
Pistol! Away, Bardolph! *[Exit Bardolph.]* Come, Pistol,
utter more to me, and withal devise something to do
thyself good. Boot, boot, Master Shallow. I know the
young king is sick for me. Let us take any man's horses;
the laws of England are at my commandment. Blessed
are they that have been my friends, and woe to my lord
chief justice!

PISTOL
Let vultures vile seize on his lungs also!
137   'Where is the life that late I led?' say they.
Why, here it is. Welcome these pleasant days!   *Exeunt.*

*

V, iv   *Enter Beadle and three or four Officers [with Hostess
               Quickly and Doll Tearsheet].*

HOSTESS No, thou arrant knave, I would to God that I
might die, that I might have thee hanged. Thou hast
drawn my shoulder out of joint.

BEADLE The constables have delivered her over to me,
5   and she shall have whipping-cheer enough, I warrant
6   her. There hath been a man or two lately killed about her.
7 DOLL Nut-hook, nut-hook, you lie. Come on, I'll tell thee
8   what, thou damned tripe-visaged rascal, an the child I

---

137 *'Where ... led'* (a snatch from an old song)
V, iv A London street   5 *whipping-cheer* a whipping for supper   6 *about
her* on her account   7 *Nut-hook* a hooked stick used in nutting   8 *tripe-
visaged* flabby-faced

now go with do miscarry, thou wert better thou hadst
struck thy mother, thou paper-faced villain.

HOSTESS O the Lord, that Sir John were come! He would
make this a bloody day to somebody. But I pray God
the fruit of her womb miscarry!

BEADLE If it do, you shall have a dozen of cushions again.
You have but eleven now. Come, I charge you both go 15
with me, for the man is dead that you and Pistol beat
amongst you. 17

DOLL I'll tell you what, you thin man in a censer, I will 18
have you as soundly swinged for this – you blue-bottle 19
rogue, you filthy famished correctioner, if you be not
swinged, I'll forswear half-kirtles. 21

BEADLE Come, come, you she knight-errant, come.

HOSTESS O God, that right should thus overcome might!
Well, of sufferance comes ease. 24

DOLL Come, you rogue, come, bring me to a justice.

HOSTESS Ay, come, you starved bloodhound.

DOLL Goodman death, goodman bones!

HOSTESS Thou atomy, thou! 28

DOLL Come, you thin thing, come, you rascal.

BEADLE Very well.   [*Exeunt.*]

*

Enter [Grooms as] strewers of rushes.   V, v
1. GROOM More rushes, more rushes.   1
2. GROOM The trumpets have sounded twice.
3. GROOM 'Twill be two o'clock ere they come from the
coronation. Dispatch, dispatch.   [*Exeunt.*]

---

15 *eleven now* (Doll has used one of the cushions to simulate pregnancy) 17
amongst you the two of you together   18 *thin . . . censer* embossed figure on
the lid of a censer, a pot for burning incense   19 *swinged* thrashed; *blue-
bottle* (the beadles wore blue coats)   21 *half-kirtles* skirts   24 *sufferance*
suffering   28 *atomy* anatomy, skeleton
V, v Before Westminster Abbey   1 *rushes* (floors were strewn with rushes
on ceremonial occasions; in this case the streets seem to have been lined
with them)

*Trumpets sound, and the King and his Train pass over
the stage. After them enter Falstaff, Shallow, Pistol,
Bardolph, and the Boy [Page].*

FALSTAFF Stand here by me, Master Robert Shallow, I
6   will make the king do you grace. I will leer upon him as
'a comes by, and do but mark the countenance that he
will give me.

PISTOL God bless thy lungs, good knight.

FALSTAFF Come here, Pistol, stand behind me. O, if I had
11   had time to have made new liveries, I would have bestowed the thousand pound I borrowed of you. But 'tis
no matter; this poor show doth better. This doth infer
the zeal I had to see him.

SHALLOW It doth so.

FALSTAFF It shows my earnestness of affection –

SHALLOW It doth so.

FALSTAFF My devotion –

SHALLOW It doth, it doth, it doth.

FALSTAFF As it were, to ride day and night, and not to de-
21   liberate, not to remember, not to have patience to shift
me –

SHALLOW It is best, certain.

FALSTAFF But to stand stained with travel, and sweating
with desire to see him, thinking of nothing else, putting
all affairs else in oblivion, as if there were nothing else to
be done but to see him.

28 PISTOL 'Tis 'semper idem,' for 'obsque hoc nihil est.'
'Tis all in every part.

SHALLOW 'Tis so, indeed.

PISTOL
My knight, I will inflame thy noble liver,
And make thee rage.
Thy Doll, and Helen of thy noble thoughts,
34   Is in base durance and contagious prison,

6 *grace* honor; *leer* glance sidewise **11** *bestowed* spent **21–22** *shift me*
change my clothes **28** *semper idem* always the same; *obsque . . . est* without
this, nothing **34** *contagious* noxious

Haled thither
By most mechanical and dirty hand.   36
Rouse up revenge from ebon den with fell Alecto's 37
   snake,
For Doll is in. Pistol speaks nought but truth.

FALSTAFF

I will deliver her.

PISTOL

There roared the sea, and trumpet-clangor sounds.
    [The trumpets sound.] Enter the King and his Train
    [, the Lord Chief Justice among them].

FALSTAFF

God save thy grace, King Hal, my royal Hal!

PISTOL

The heavens thee guard and keep, most royal imp of 42
   fame!

FALSTAFF

God save thee, my sweet boy!

KING

My lord chief justice, speak to that vain man.

CHIEF JUSTICE

Have you your wits? Know you what 'tis you speak?

FALSTAFF

My king! My Jove! I speak to thee, my heart!

KING

I know thee not, old man. Fall to thy prayers.
How ill white hairs become a fool and jester!
I have long dreamed of such a kind of man,
So surfeit-swelled, so old, and so profane,
But, being awaked, I do despise my dream.
Make less thy body hence, and more thy grace.   53
Leave gormandizing. Know the grave doth gape
For thee thrice wider than for other men.
Reply not to me with a fool-born jest.

---

36 *mechanical* workman's, base   **37** *ebon* black; *Alecto* one of the Furies   **42**
royal imp young son of the royal house   **53** *hence* henceforth

Presume not that I am the thing I was,
For God doth know, so shall the world perceive,
That I have turned away my former self.
So will I those that kept me company.
When thou dost hear I am as I have been,
Approach me, and thou shalt be as thou wast,
The tutor and the feeder of my riots.
Till then, I banish thee, on pain of death,
As I have done the rest of my misleaders,
Not to come near our person by ten mile.
67   For competence of life I will allow you,
That lack of means enforce you not to evils.
And, as we hear you do reform yourselves,
We will, according to your strengths and qualities,
Give you advancement. Be it your charge, my lord,
72   To see performed the tenor of our word.
Set on.   *[Exeunt the King and his Train.]*

FALSTAFF Master Shallow, I owe you a thousand pound.

SHALLOW Yea, marry, Sir John, which I beseech you to
let me have home with me.

FALSTAFF That can hardly be, Master Shallow. Do not
you grieve at this. I shall be sent for in private to him.
Look you, he must seem thus to the world. Fear not
your advancements; I will be the man yet that shall
make you great.

SHALLOW I cannot well perceive how, unless you should
give me your doublet and stuff me out with straw. I
beseech you, good Sir John, let me have five hundred of
my thousand.

FALSTAFF Sir, I will be as good as my word. This that
87   you heard was but a color.

SHALLOW A color that I fear you will die in, Sir John.

89 FALSTAFF Fear no colors. Go with me to dinner. Come,
Lieutenant Pistol, come, Bardolph. I shall be sent for

67 *competence of life* allowance for support   72 *tenor* intention   87 *color*
pretense   89 *colors* enemy

soon at night.   91
    Enter [the Lord Chief] Justice and Prince John [of
    Lancaster, with Officers].

CHIEF JUSTICE
  Go, carry Sir John Falstaff to the Fleet.   92
  Take all his company along with him.

FALSTAFF
  My lord, my lord –

CHIEF JUSTICE
  I cannot now speak. I will hear you soon.
  Take them away.

PISTOL
  'Si fortuna me tormenta, spero contenta.'   97
               Exeunt [all but Prince John and the
                            Chief Justice].

LANCASTER
  I like this fair proceeding of the king's.
  He hath intent his wonted followers   99
  Shall all be very well provided for,
  But all are banished till their conversations
  Appear more wise and modest to the world.

CHIEF JUSTICE
  And so they are.

LANCASTER
  The king hath called his parliament, my lord.

CHIEF JUSTICE
  He hath.

LANCASTER
  I will lay odds that, ere this year expire,
  We bear our civil swords and native fire   107
  As far as France. I heard a bird so sing,
  Whose music, to my thinking, pleased the king.
  Come, will you hence?   *[Exeunt.]*

---

91 *soon at night* early in the evening   **92** *Fleet* a famous London prison   **97**
Si . . . contenta if fortune torments me, hope contents me   **99** *wonted*
accustomed   **107** *civil swords* swords used in civil wars

Epi.   EPILOGUE [Spoken by a Dancer]

First my fear, then my curtsy, last my speech. My fear is, your displeasure; my curtsy, my duty; and my speech, to beg your pardons. If you look for a good speech now, you
4 undo me, for what I have to say is of mine own making,
5 and what indeed I should say will, I doubt, prove mine own marring. But to the purpose, and so to the venture. Be it known to you, as it is very well, I was lately here in the end
8 of a displeasing play, to pray your patience for it and to promise you a better. I meant indeed to pay you with this,
10 which, if like an ill venture it come unluckily home, I break, and you, my gentle creditors, lose. Here I promised you I would be and here I commit my body to your mercies.
13 Bate me some and I will pay you some and, as most debtors do, promise you infinitely.

If my tongue cannot entreat you to acquit me, will you command me to use my legs? And yet that were but light payment, to dance out of your debt. But a good conscience will make any possible satisfaction, and so would I. All the gentlewomen here have forgiven me. If the gentlemen will not, then the gentlemen do not agree with the gentlewomen, which was never seen before in such an assembly.

One word more, I beseech you. If you be not too much cloyed with fat meat, our humble author will continue the story, with Sir John in it, and make you merry with fair Katherine of France. Where, for anything I know, Falstaff shall die of a sweat, unless already 'a be killed with your
27 hard opinions, for Oldcastle died a martyr, and this is not the man. My tongue is weary. When my legs are too, I will bid you good night, and so kneel down before you, but, indeed, to pray for the queen.

Epi. 4 *undo* ruin **5** *doubt* fear **8** *displeasing play* (this play has never been identified) **10** *break* am bankrupt **13** *Bate me some* relieve me of some of my debts **27-28** *Oldcastle . . . man* (In the Henry IV plays Falstaff was originally called Oldcastle. Objection was made to the use of this name since the historical Sir John Oldcastle, who was executed for treason in 1417, was in the sixteenth century honored as a martyr in the cause of Protestantism. Here Shakespeare is saying 'My character was not intended as the historical Oldcastle.')